WELDING

A PRACTICAL GUIDE TO JOINING METALS

WELDING

A PRACTICAL GUIDE TO JOINING METALS

Martin and Ed Thaddeus

THE CROWOOD PRESS

First published in 2010 by
The Crowood Press Ltd
Ramsbury, Marlborough
Wiltshire SN8 2HR

www.crowood.com

British Library Cataloguing-in-Publication Data
A catalogue record for this book is available from the British Library.

ISBN 978 1 84797 189 0

Printed and bound in Singapore by Craft Print International

Contents

Anyone practising metalwork must take responsibility for their own safety.

Introduction

This book is written as a practical guide for the hobbyist who wishes to join metal. We are primarily concerned with welding, brazing and soldering, but will also discuss the alternatives, such as mechanical fixings and adhesives. What distinguishes soldering from brazing? What do we mean by pure fusion? Mechanical, electrical and aesthetic considerations must be weighed up, and a compromise may be needed to get the best for your particular project. What indeed are the alternatives to welding, such as mechanical fixings and chemical fixings and adhesives?

Many interests require metal to be joined in many ways, and while the principles for welding are essentially the same, the techniques best suited to replacing a wing on a classic car are not necessarily the best for mounting a stone on a fine silver ring. So whether you are aiming to work with stained-glass or restore tractors, it pays to become familiar with the range of methods at your disposal before deciding which path to go down.

The workspace chapter will help you set up an appropriate place to do welding and alert you to the potential dangers that are inherent to the processes and equipment involved. You cannot be vigilant to unknown threats, but it is useful to become familiar with any process before trying it at home. Anyone choosing to practise any form of craft or metalwork must take responsibility for their own safety and the safety of anyone else who might be affected by their actions.

The spectrum of processes runs from non-fusion techniques such as soft soldering, through brazing, to pure fusion techniques such as Tig (tungsten inert gas) and gas welding, which are by nature more industrial. The chapters cover each of the selected processes in depth.

Soft soldering is used for electrical joining and sheetwork, as well as specialist areas such as stained-glass and terraria. Silver soldering or hard soldering, while traditionally a jewellery technique, has recently crept into car repair. Aluminium, a difficult material to work with, has its own chapter describing materials that have recently come onto the market claiming to join aluminium and its alloys with only a butane torch.

Gas welding appeals to the craftsman, and in the hands of a master it is poetry. The welding story begins with the chapter on oxy-acetylene fusion welding, the industry standard for the motor trade for decades until the Mig (metal inert gas) welder took over in the 1980s. In the gas chapter we also discuss bronzework, which is stronger than solder and easier than true welding, and best carried out with oxy-acetylene or oxy-propane gear. A more recent option covered here is Tig brazing, which has so much in common with oxy-acetylene welding.

Resistance spot welding has many advantages over other forms of welding, especially in the area of vehicle repair and restoration. This was the original method used to construct the vast majority of motor vehicles after the Second World War, and is also used in joining sheet metal and in boxwork.

The entry-level welding method is MMA (manual arc welding) or stick welding, which has been largely superseded by the use of Mig. The newer 'inverter' machines are smoother and easier to use. Mig welding utilizes an arc formed between a live torch and an earthed workpiece. Relatively cheap and easy, Mig is the mainstay of welding for the enthusiast in the field of bodywork and car restoration. Tig welding is more difficult than Mig, but it can produce the highest quality of weld, and the

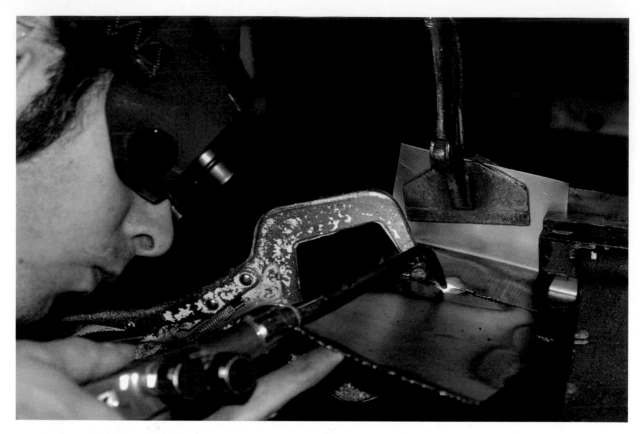

new inverter welders have brought Tig into the domestic market.

In the next section we consider a wide range of popular techniques for creating joints, beginning with alternatives to welding. Because of its distinct nature we cover plumbing in a separate chapter on the principles, techniques and materials for the soldering of copper pipework. This is followed by the mechanics of forming a joint with regard to the problems of heat dissipation and distortion, and a chapter on how to create joints in box-section tubes and bars. Finally this book would not be complete without a look at our own specialty: panel and sheet metal techniques as they apply to vehicle bodywork.

No book, however comprehensive, can cover all of the risks or predict every eventuality. You should take advice before fabricating or modifying any safety-critical component. Cast alloy wheels, for example,

Gas welding.

should not be repaired or modified using any of the techniques shown in this book, as uneven thermal disruption will cause localized softening which could lead to failure under load. Safety is very much a state of mind, and while we will give as much instruction as possible there is no substitute for learning first-hand from an experienced practitioner.

We would like to thank the following people and companies for their help in producing this book: Geoff Newby at Weld UK Ltd. for technical help and advice; Sealey Power Products, Colin Wright at Crawley Welding Supplies, Parweld UK and BOC Gases Ltd. We extend special thanks to antique metal specialist Peter Powell for his expert help with the chapter on silver soldering, and to Dresda Motorcycles in West Sussex for their practical demonstrations.

MMA.

CHAPTER 1

What Exactly Is Welding?

What do we mean by soldering, brazing and welding? These terms are not as clearly defined from one another as many imagine, and a large degree of overlap and confusion exists between them.

Soldering is commonly perceived to be a fairly domestic process, while brazing is inherently more industrial. In truth what separates soldering from brazing is simply the temperature at which the alloy bonding agent melts. Under this definition then, what we call silver 'soldering' should correctly be termed silver 'brazing'.

Another common misunderstanding is that brass alloy is exclusively employed in brazing. The term brazing can also refer to the brazier or torch. In aluminium brazing we use a wire made from an aluminium alloy, which melts at a lower temperature than the parent metal being joined. Traditionally, brazing does employ a brass alloy wire which, when heated, is flowed into the joint by capillary action, in much the same way as soft solder. Silver solder can contain anything from as little as 2 per cent silver up to 92.5 per cent, which is sterling and therefore hallmark-able. The range of silver solders has a broad range of melting points.

Welding in the true sense of the word is the term used when two pieces of metal are fused together without adding any foreign alloy. In the case of gas and Tig welding, we can achieve pure fusion by simply heating a localized area of two pieces until they flow together; a filler wire of the same material is used to bridge any holes only where needed. With Mig welding a continuous deposition of new metal is an inherent part of the process.

What then are brass welding and bronze welding? It is important to point out that neither of these

Work set-up for soldering.

methods is actually 'welding'. Brass welding, as opposed to brazing, is where we build up the brass filler as a shoulder or fillet to reinforce the joint. Bronze welding is the same process, but using a filler wire made of a bronze alloy rather than one of brass. Brass and bronze are differentiated only by their copper content; bronze wire will tend to melt at a higher temperature than brass.

THE PRINCIPLES OF JOINING METAL

The principles of joining metal with weld and braze are largely governed and limited by two factors – penetration and surface area. Penetration refers to the depth to which the new material mixes with the old and also the degree to which the heat disrupts or denatures it.

Soft soldering is used to join electrical components where brazing or welding would most likely simply destroy them. To promote a sound union, we rely on the area of surface contact and the capillary attraction of the wet solder between the two sides of our joint. A bolt passed through two pieces of metal would be a good example of total penetration without heat disruption. The bolthead or any washers used would govern the surface area that this fixing acted upon.

In the perfect weld we would see two pieces of steel fuse to become one homogenous item. While we will always aim to create this situation, the truth is that some flaw or compromise will inevitably be present. Pure fusion may exist at the actual point of weld, but the surrounding metal will inevitably also be affected by the heat involved in the process.

The area immediately surrounding the weld, known as the heat affected zone (HAZ) or the area of thermal disruption, is heated but not to the point

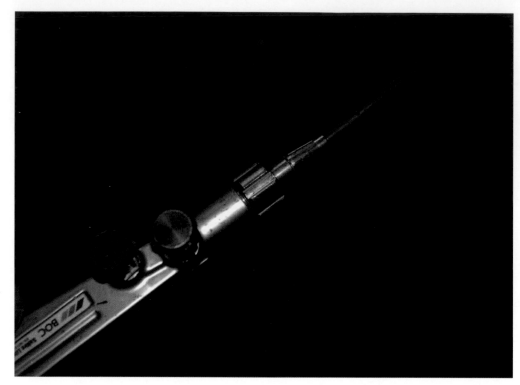

Left: Oxy-acetylene torch.

Right: Spot welder.

of melting. The effect is one of 'normalizing', which is to say, the metal's crystals will take on the random arrangement found in annealing. In the case of the resistance spot welder, this property allows us to easily break the ring of metal surrounding each weld by simply wiggling it back and forth.

Hammering or dressing the weld can be used to restore surface tension or temper, but in the case of Mig the grade of steel used to make the wire will often be harder than the grade of steel being joined.

Structural integrity may be adversely affected by a localized area which is harder or softer than its surrounding metal. If you were building a wind turbine or an aeroplane wing, the result might be catastrophic. Even for our more domestic projects, this has to remain a consideration. As an example, a captive nut behind a vehicle panel will often be sited on a penny washer. The job of the washer is to act as 'spreader plate' and dissipate the load to avoid any peak stress that might pull the nut through. When mounting the washer you would be well advised not to weld completely around it, as the lack of surface tension in the HAZ could leave this considerably weakened. The weld here is used only

to locate the washer and prevent turning. (This situation will be found when dealing with car seatbelt anchorage.) Vehicle manufacturers frown upon the use of Mig welds in some repair applications, on the grounds that they are too 'tough' or resistant to deformation under impact conditions.

THE WELDING PROCESS
Why do we need a flux?

Most metals oxidize, which is to say, the surface will attract the formation of an oxide layer. Oxides tend to be rather harder than the parent metal and will usually interfere with any other substance bonding to it. A flux strips any oxides and prevents the formation of new ones during the joining process. Fluxes will in some cases improve 'wetting' – that is, they will alter the surface tension of the liquid metal to help it flow.

Why do we need a shielding gas?

In much the same way as a flux, shielding gases displace oxygen from the welding field to prevent the formation of oxides, which would otherwise impede

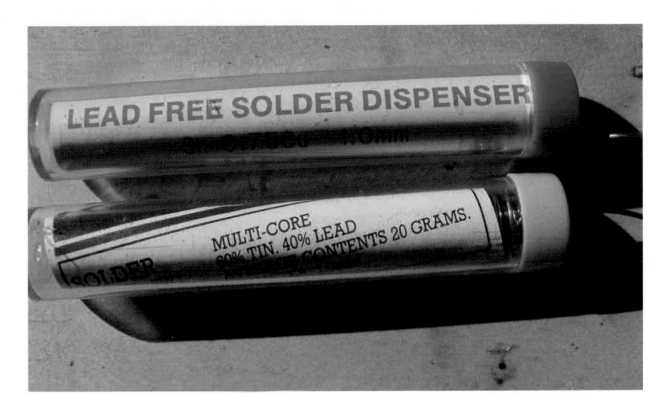

bonding. In MMA arc welding and in gasless Mig, the shielding gas is held as a flux on (or in) the consumable wire and is released by the arc itself. In Tig welding the argon shielding gas also helps to keep the tungsten electrode cool, which helps to prolong its life.

Which method?

Just to confuse things further, it must be understood that soldering can be carried out with an 'iron', which can be electrically heated or gas powered or can indeed simply be heated in a forge. Larger soldering jobs such as plumbing work more usually involve a blowtorch. Oxy-acetylene gas welding gear is commonly used to carry out brazing exercises including silver-soldering. Electric tongs can also be employed to braze, as can an industrial oven. Tig welding, though usually a pure fusion method, can also be used to braze, and top of the range Mig equipment can also be rigged with a brazing wire to join high-tensile steel panels.

Over the years, many methods of welding have been developed and employed in industry, and without doubt many more will evolve in the years to come. Most of these will probably never impact upon the amateur. It is unlikely that laser welding will ever come into the domestic market, but most would probably have said the same about Tig welding just twenty years ago. Anyone interested in the joining of metal for whatever reason would do well to keep an eye on developments in welding technology.

PROMOTING STRENGTH

These are some of the tricks and techniques used to promote strength in a welded joint. Many are common or transferable to brazing or braze welding.

Gap and Fill

In order to promote penetration and therefore fusion, we will often leave a gap in a butt joint or chamfer its edges. We then replace the missing material with filler rod or MIG wire. Webs and shoulders of weld are also commonly employed to reinforce a joint.

Sleeves and Straps

Another technique is to insert a sleeve or strap

inside or behind a join – this allows for hotter and more confident welding. Sleeves and straps can also be used to help align or reinforce a joint.

Successive Runs of Weld

When forming a fillet joint it is worth noting that a concave weld is stronger about its centre than a convex one, though most would agree that the convex weld is the more attractive, and will usually be the result of a hotter weld with better flow of the new material.

When building up weld material in a joint, we must pay a little attention to the order in which we place each run. For example, a corner fillet might be joined with a bead of weld which is then covered with two successive passes. The second pass should be aimed at the bottom of the initial run, and the third built onto this. If we were to place the second bead at the top, it would likely result in an overhang which would be difficult to bond further material to. At worst, the poor fusion of the third pass could

Turbo-weld mini welding set.

leave a hollow within the joint. An alternative to running parallel beads or weld is to zig-zag over the initial weld.

It is not unusual to use tack welds or a small bead or weld at a relatively low power or heat when initially fixing a fillet or V-butt joint. These tentative welds are then consumed into successive passes of more confident weld – which might be hotter or, in the case of MMA, formed from a larger diameter electrode. The joint can then be turned over and the original root run given what is known as a sealing run.

Soldering and Brazing

This philosophy continues into soldering and brazing, but as actual fusion is not achieved we rely more on the area of contact to give us our strength.

SILVER AND GOLD

Lead/tin solder will alloy to the surface of silver and if reheated can alloy deeper to form a nasty grey pitted material which is virtually unworkable; this may need to be cut out and replaced.

Gold is soldered with gold of a lesser quality, that is to say 24-carat can be soldered with 18-carat, which in turn is soldered with 15 and so on. These alloys of gold will alloy themselves with the base metal to some degree.

Soft lead/tin solders can be thought of as adhesives, in much the same way as a glue which bonds only onto the very surface of the metal. Butt joints are not possible with soft solder, so an overlap or lip is required.

Capillary brazed joints are stronger than solder, but still rely on the amount of surface area to govern strength.

Braze weld and bronze weld don't rely entirely on capillary action or overlap, but employ a shoulder of new material that is solidly bonded to the surface of both pieces.

Studding

This is a method of increasing penetration by drilling and tapping a hole into the face to be repaired; into this is screwed a stud. The stud is then welded in and incorporated into successive runs of weld material.

Buttering

This is the term given to layers of weld that are applied to each face of a joint before the actual joining. In the case of cast-iron, use a buttering of pure or high nickel rod followed by filling with much cheaper mild steel material.

Creating a Mig stud.

A fire blanket and fire extinguisher are crucial pieces of safety equipment in the workshop.

CHAPTER 2

The Workspace

Selecting an appropriate place to work is crucial if you are to get the best results in the safest manner. All of the metal joining methods and techniques shown in this book come with some inherent risk. Simple domestic soldering, for example, poses hazards from the hot iron and the fumes, which result from use of both the solder and its flux.

Electrical soldering or stained-glass work involving an iron may indeed be carried out at home – preferably in a hobby room, garage or shed. At a push you can use the kitchen table. But be certain that the work area will not be disrupted by children or pets. A proper stand for the iron is essential, as is a robust electrical supply – never use a coiled extension lead or one which cannot cope easily with the electrical load.

All soldering will involve noxious fumes from the solder and flux. The simplest of DIY solders come with the flux running through them as a core. Do not be fooled into thinking that any fumes are harmless – consider fitting extraction or wearing a suitable mask.

Work only on a stable bench or table, and pay heed to your own balance. Good, even, ambient lighting is also important for safe and accurate work – daylight bulbs and tubes will reduce fatigue and encourage well-being in the work area.

THE WORKSHOP

Processes that are more industrial in nature, such as Mig welding, cannot be carried out on the dining table due to the shower of white-hot sparks that issue from the blinding arc of the torch. But even the Mig poses some risks that are less than obvious. The machine itself is heavy and unstable due to the gas bottle; it has a mains flex which poses a tripping hazard; and the argon shielding gas is an 'oxygen depletor' – which is to say that though not actually toxic, it will displace oxygen from the work area which can then lead to asphyxia.

Many metal-joining methods involve intense heat, so combustion is the first risk to consider. Ventilation is the next consideration. Ideally a workshop in which welding is carried out would be constructed entirely of brick, concrete and steel. The floors would be perfectly flat and the workshop would feature large skylights and windows, and would be fitted with flameproof lighting. Benches would be of heavy steel construction, and no flammable materials would be present. However, in reality it is more likely that you will be welding in a lock-up or a corner of a workshop in which more general activities are taking place.

Shown overleaf is a typical small-time workshop located in a converted cowshed on a farm. The building is of brick/block construction with concrete trusses holding a tiled roof with a skylight. The floor slopes badly and is far from smooth. The shop is fitted with serious industrial lighting, including low-level 'oblique' light on the walls – all tubes are of the daylight variety. As can be seen, several cars are in the building, and as such, several people might be working at once. The building itself poses very little fire risk, but the cars and various bits of trim randomly scattered and stored about the place, do.

CONSTRUCTION

If the workshop has wooden sides and rafters they need to be watched, as a stray spark might lead to slow 'smouldering', which can flare up many hours after the welding has stopped. (It is standard practice within the motor trade that all welding or

Professional welding shop: safe construction and orderly working.

flame-based work be stopped at least half an hour before the close of play – this allows for any unseen smouldering to become apparent.) Check – is there a second exit? Does the roof leak?

PROXIMITY TO OTHER BUILDINGS OR PEOPLE

In the event of fire, would it pose a risk to other structures or the people in them? Likewise, fumes and noise may prove to be a nuisance. In an emergency, can gas bottles be safely removed away from other buildings, people and animals?

LOCATION/ACCESS

Can you safely enter and exit the building? Can you raise the alarm? Can the emergency services access the building?

LAYOUT

Is the workshop divided into bays? Are you going to be hemmed in by benches or other cars? Will sparks from your work play over other cars or stored items? Is there any solvent/paint/petrol on the premises? Is the fire exit blocked?

UTILITIES

Do you have power and water? What about a phone line or mobile network? Garbage disposal? Failure to remove rubbish will lead to a build-up of bags. A stray rag or paper towel under the bench can easily lead to a surprise flame-up. Overloading the electrical supply can also cause the cables to overheat.

LIGHTING

Never underestimate the importance of good lighting, but bear in mind that once you pull down the welding visor, the balance of lighting is quite different. You may find that some overhead lighting will interfere with a 'self-darkening' visor. Natural daylight is usually the best light to work by.

Above: Typical welding environment: safe building and chaotic activity.

Right: Flat construction area in pro shop.

Coherent and safe metal storage.

Extraction system to remove noxious welding fumes.

Safety is a state of mind: be aware of your surroundings.

Grinding and associated processes also pose risks.

Worst case scenario: disasters are rare, but vigilance is key.

Spark gun must be used to ignite gas torch – matches and cigarette lighters are not safe.

VENTILATION/EXTRACTION

Brazing and welding will inevitably generate fumes and in the case of Mig and Tig, there will also be a risk of oxygen depletion due to the shielding gas. Many of the other processes associated with welding – such as grinding – produce hazardous by-products. Portable extraction/filter machines are available. Do not direct fumes towards other people or buildings. Some welding helmets offer the option of a belt-mounted filter, which blows clean air through the mask and over the face.

Metal fume fever, due to inhalation of zinc, and delayed lung damage caused by ozone are a risk from some processes. Do not underestimate these potential problems.

HEATING

People make silly mistakes and slip-ups when they are cold. Metal objects are difficult to handle and more difficult to weld when cold or damp. Welding equipment and power tools do not like to be stored in very cold or damp conditions.

SAFETY EQUIPMENT

FIRE EXTINGUISHERS

CO_2 and powder. A domestic 'squirty bottle' filled with water will do for most minor flames before they take hold. A squirty is also very good for damping down areas around where welding will take place – this prevents fires before they can start.

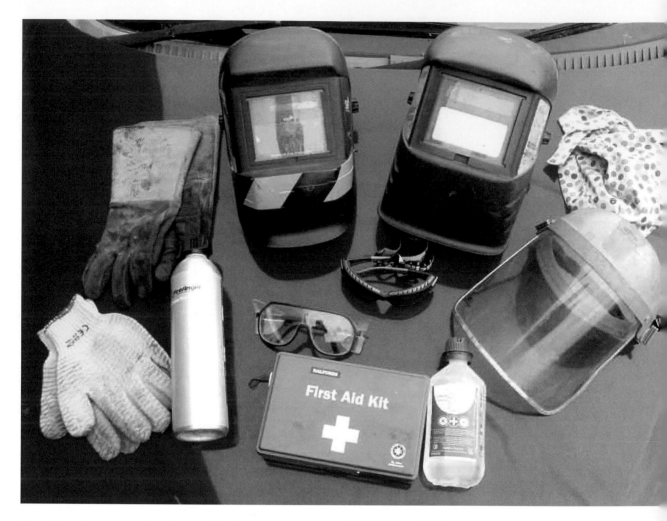

Essential safety gear: goggles, visors, welding helmet, bandanna, first aid kit, eyewash etc.

A fire-blanket is also essential; some are suitable for covering flammable items to prevent ignition, while others are single use and kept for emergency use only. Water buckets, damp cloths and hose pipes are also to be considered.

FIRST AID KIT
A comprehensive first aid kit and the basic knowledge of how to use it, are obviously a must. Injuries from power tools, sharp edges and hot objects must be catered for. A good eyewash is also essential. Plan ahead how best you might get an injured party to hospital.

WELDING SCREEN
A screen will protect anyone else in the room from the potentially damaging arc – it will also keep your grinding-sparks off other cars.

PERSONAL SAFETY

VISOR OR WELDING HELMET
Safety goggles or better still a full-face visor are essential for working with power tools such as drills and grinders which are widely used in metal work. Darkened glass goggles are required for any work which involves looking at a bright flame. The self-darkening mask is now the standard for work involving an arc such as Mig or Tig. EU compliant models can be bought for less than £50 and will improve your welding ability greatly, as well as

*Left: Cotton overalls
and safety boots.*

*Above: Soldering iron
and stand.*

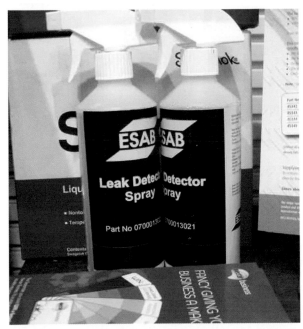

Leak detector spray: take no chances.

Acetylene is an unstable highly explosive gas.

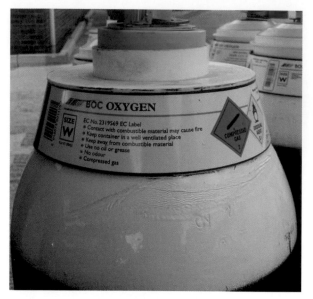

Oxygen will actively encourage combustion.

Argon CO_2 is an asphyxiant and is heavier than air.

All gases are pressurized and are held in heavy bottles with brass valves.

Electrical welding gear has its own set of hazards.

Organized welding station with everything to hand.

giving you back your left hand. Welding masks come in a variety of shades to suit particular processes. Better masks are adjustable to cover a wide range of tasks. Consult you supplier to ensure the mask you buy is the correct one.

OVERALLS
These should be made of cotton and preferably flame-proof. Fire-retardant fabrics are often no longer protected after washing, so check with your supplier.

HAT
A good welding hat or bandana will protect against burns to the head. In cold weather it is tempting to wear an ordinary hat, which may be highly flammable.

GLOVES
Gloves and gauntlets will protect the hands against spatter, but may also lessen sensitivity. Gloves are essential for handling sheet metal and hot objects – they will also protect against radiation from Tig welding. Cotton gloves are also recommended in the Tig process to prevent contamination of cleaned metal to be welded.

FOOTWEAR
It is generally understood that safety boots are a must, but in practice many panel beaters prefer to

wear softer shoes which can be removed quickly in the event of a stray spark fizzing between the toes. Failure to wear safety footwear is at your own risk.

BREATHING MASK
Charcoal-impregnated masks are available at low cost; these will filter out many organic particulates.

Real life welding application: please assess risks.

Specialist formulation solders for particular jobs.

CHAPTER 3

Soft Soldering

Soft soldering is a method of joining pieces of metal by heating an alloy of (traditionally) tin and lead. This type of solder has a melting point which is considerably lower than the metals which it is used to join, and relies on capillary action and surface area to create strength and water tightness within a join.

WHAT METALS CAN IT JOIN?

Soft soldering is most commonly used to join brass, copper and steel. Soft solder can also be used to join dissimilar metals. Aluminium can also be soldered, but this is a slightly different process (*see* Chapter 5).

WHAT IS IT USED FOR?

Soft soldering is generally used for electrical joints and plumbing work, as well as for stained-glass windows or sheet copper/brass construction such as terraria work. Each of these applications demands a different approach, as do the various methods of heating which may be brought to bear.

Soft solder is also used as a temporary fixing method in some panel repair techniques, as reheating the solder will break the bonds which hold it to the substrate metal. The ability to de-solder a joint is often put to good use in electrical work. Very low-temperature (bismuth) solders can then be used to re-solder a connection without the risk of damage to any nearby joints.

ALSO KNOWN AS?

Lead soldering, tin soldering or tinning.

HOW DOES IT WORK?

Heat

Heating of the solder may be by means of an iron, which can be either electrical, gas-powered or simply heated in a brazier or hearth. Soldering 'irons', which are heated by a flame, are often made of copper and should more correctly be called 'soldering coppers'. For plumbing work a blowtorch is usually employed.

Solder

Soft soldering involves a range of solders which melt below 400°C, which distinguishes the process from hard (silver) soldering and brazing. Originally tin/lead solders were used, but lead-free solders are now becoming popular for safety reasons – these melt at 250°C.

General purpose flux and heavy duty solder for copper work.

Mapp gas torch for application demanding a lot of heat.

Hobby shops stock a wide range of soldering equipment.

Domestic iron with stand.

Mini welding torch can be used for small soldering jobs.

Mini butane torch is refilled with lighter fuel and provides very quick soldering heat.

A 'solder-sucker' or de-soldering pump can be used to remove excess hot solder.

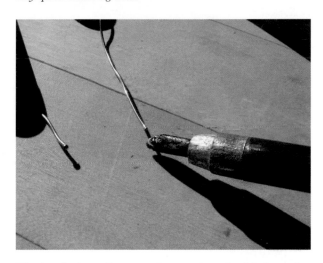

Tinning the iron. Some say that any iron should always be kept tinned.

Flux

All soldering work demands a flux that cleans the area, impedes the formation of oxides and prevents contamination from interfering with the bonding of the solder to the substrate surface. The flux will also improve 'wetting', by reducing the surface tension of the solder as it heats. More reactive fluxes may need to be cleaned off the work after the joint has been made. Domestic solders often feature a core of flux within the solder itself. Separate fluxes may be applied as a powder, paste or liquid. Pre-cleaning with an acid or alkali bath might also be considered in some cases. All fluxes should be regarded as toxic, as should their fumes.

RISKS / SAFETY CONSIDERATIONS

- Mains-operated irons will employ a lead which poses a tripping hazard.
- Gas-powered irons and torches use pressurized gas.

A BEGINNER'S GUIDE TO SOFT SOLDERING

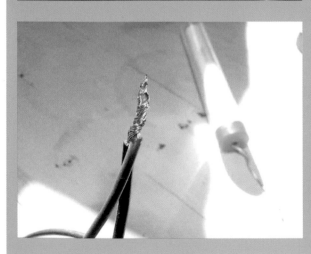

This exercise gives practice in soft soldering a typical electrical connection with a domestic electric soldering iron.

METHOD 1

The trick with soldering is to heat both pieces equally. This may mean heating one piece more than the other, if it's bigger or made of a less conductive metal, in order to balance out the heat distribution.

To heat the metal simply hold the tip of your hot soldering iron to it in the area you want to solder. After a moment to let the heat soak in a bit, feed the wire in at the tip of your iron – if your piece is hot enough it should flow onto it; if not it will simply melt into a little round blob. Ideally what you want to see in your solder joint is that there is no roundness to the solder; it should stick to both pieces and flow between them like a cobweb.

If it all goes wrong then you can always reheat it and remove some of the solder, and start over (a 'solder-sucker' is a pump for removing excess material).

METHOD 2

An alternative way to get a solder joint is a technique called pre-tinning or tinning – this is simply melting the solder onto each piece separately and then heating them both together, so the solder from both fuses. This is often a much quicker and easier way to solder two pieces with different heat soaks. Always bear in mind the old adage about a sound mechanical joint being the basis of a sound electrical joint, but also watch out not to overheat any of the components. Various things can be used as heat sinks to protect delicate items – pliers, clips and bits of foil might do – or you could invest in some 'Coldfront' cream.

Some people will tell you that the tip of any iron should be given a coating of solder from new and that it should always be tinned, if it is to work well. Others say that the tip should be thoroughly cleaned before each use.

JOINTING METHOD 1:
SOLDERING BOTH CONTACTS AT ONCE

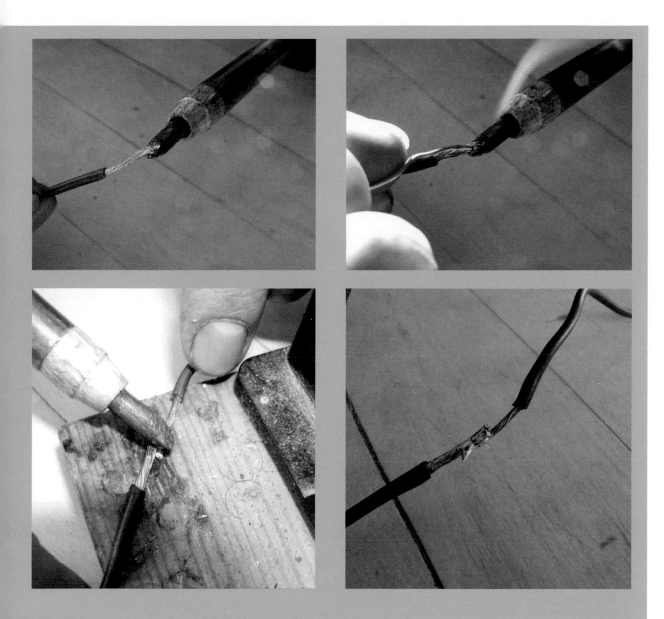

JOINTING METHOD 2:
TINNING THE CONTACT INDIVIDUALLY BEFORE
BRINGING TOGETHER AND HEATING

Above: Regular glass uses straight cames.

Far left: Tiffany glass can be formed onto complex shapes.

Left an example of terraria work.

Traditional stained-glass work used lead cames.

- All solders and fluxes are toxic, as are their fumes, regardless of newer formulations not containing lead.
- Heat soak in metal objects can be deceptive, and many soldering operations require more hands than one person possesses.

SPECIAL USES

Stained-Glass Work

Traditionally, stained-glass was held in strips of lead known as 'cames'. These were joined using a lead/tin solder with hot iron or copper, which would have been heated in a hearth or brazier. Cames come in two varieties: C-section, for around the

Coldfront cream can be used to protect against heat damage.

periphery of the window; and H-section that sits between two pieces of glass. Lead came can be hardened by drawing, which is to say one end is held in a vice while the other is pulled. This increase in hardness is at the cost of increased brittleness, and is not universally approved of. Additional strength can also be gained from horizontal steel rods which can be hidden within the design of the panels; these are held in place by copper wire.

Traditional colouring may be obtained from metallic salts within the actual glass or possibly painted onto the surface before firing in a kiln. Newer non-toxic translucent paints are available for those not worried about authenticity.

Tiffany Glass Work

This method of joining decorative glass uses a copper foil, which is wrapped over the edges of each piece and then soldered along its length. The 'Tiffany' method allows for the construction of large free-standing objects such as screens, as well as the fabulous three-dimensional lampshades that made it famous. Larger items will be seen to have supporting steel or copper work between or around the glass panels.

The obvious risk here is that the glass can be heated to the point of breaking. Copper is a very good conductor of heat, which should protect against this problem. Modelling clay or other mate-

rials can be used to hold the work while it is being soldered. Pre-tinning the individual foil edges will greatly improve the quality of joint, and make tacking easy. A second pass of the iron will allow further solder to be flowed along the joint.

A trawl of the internet will reveal no end of Tiffany-style work, some of which is cheaply made in the Far East. Original items from the Tiffany workshop reach huge values, but as the techniques used to produce them are essentially simple, there is no reason why the dedicated craftsman or woman should not create something special of their own.

Terraria Work

Somewhat out of fashion, the terrarium or mini-greenhouse has a history which peaked in the Victorian era. Traditionally the terrarium was constructed from extruded brass sections into which the thin glass panels were set. The brasswork would be joined where it intersects with a soft lead solder, using an iron which would have been heated using a brazier. In much the same way as Tiffany work, the metal edging is relied upon to keep the heat safely away from the glass. Once the construction was complete the glazing was sealed using a waterproof putty; this has the added quality of increasing the rigidity of the panel. Individual glass panels, which could range from plain to exquisitely ornate, would be made up separately on a flat table before being mounted into the structural framework. Plinths could be of hardwood or stonework.

Both original and new terraria can sell for large amounts of money, which reflects the craftsmanship required to produce a fine example. The Tiffany method of construction can also be applied to terraria, either to make up panels which would be fitted into a brass frame or to build the entire structure.

Brass and Copper Sheetwork and Construction

For generations pots, pans, buckets and fuel tanks have been fabricated from thin metal sheet and soldered to produce watertight seams. All seams would usually be overlapped or rolled together and the solder applied using tongs, irons or sometimes in an oven. Clamps, jigs and presses would also have been employed to aid the construction process. Today it is not acceptable to use lead solder on any vessel which is to be used in food production.

Likewise the use of many traditional metals and manufacturing methods is questionable in light of current knowledge.

Classic motor vehicle radiator repair is an area where knowledge of traditional techniques is a posi-tive bonus. Brass radiator cores are available; these are fitted to an endplate and then between top and bottom tanks, by means of a lead solder which is safe within the normal working temperature of the engine. This work would usually involve a blowtorch.

*This old silver bracelet, found in an attic, has been
constructed using silver soldering.*

CHAPTER 4

Silver Soldering

Silver solder or hard solder is a method of joining metal with a solder containing silver. It is distinguished from soft soldering by a melting point greater than 400°C and is therefore more correctly called silver brazing.

WHAT METALS CAN IT JOIN?

Silver, copper, brass, bronze, steel, gold and most of the things we as amateurs might wish to work with, except aluminium. This process can be used to join dissimilar metals.

WHAT IS IT USED FOR?

Silver soldering is the staple of jewellery work and is widely used in the fabrication, repair and restoration of bronzes, castings and statuary. It has recently been adopted by the motor repair trade. With the wide range of solders and metals that can be joined by this process, the scope of applications is endless.

ALSO KNOWN AS?

Hard solder and silver brazing.

HOW DOES IT WORK?

Heat

The heat for the process will usually be provided by a blowtorch, the size of which will be governed by the size of the job. Oxy-acetylene can also be used as the heat source in some cases if care is taken not to overheat the job.

Specialist metal workers will sometime employ a micro-welder, which is a mains-powered machine that generates hydrogen and oxygen from water by means of electrolysis. The gases are pumped at low pressure to a very small torch, where they are burned to produce a fine flame with a very high temperature.

The Turbo-weld Oxy/Mapp gas kit supplied by Welduk comes with a heating nozzle and five micro nozzles, making it suitable for fine jewellery work and dentistry applications.

Solders

A wide range of solders is available. These are known by their hardness, which usually also governs their melting points. Grades such as extra easy, easy, hard, extra hard and enamelling are supplied as wires, ribbons and rods. Many of these solders are 'hallmark-able' which is to say they contain at least 92.5 per cent silver – surprisingly the silver content does not necessarily govern the melting point. Ribbons of solder are commonly split several times lengthwise before being cut to form tiny squares called paillons.

When carrying out repair work, it is usual to use a solder with the lowest melting point that you can get away with. This will lessen the risk of causing damage to the piece. When constructing jewellery, it is standard practice to start with a harder solder and perform subsequent tasks using gradually softer ones, so as not to undo previous joins. Enamelling grade solder is designed to be able to withstand firing in a kiln without softening. In many cases a solder will require a higher temperature to melt it a second time – this allows further joints to be made using the same material without damage to previous work.

Silver is a precious metal and as such the cost of materials will fluctuate and at times be prohibitive. Some solder rods are also available only in pack

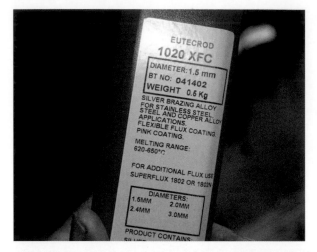

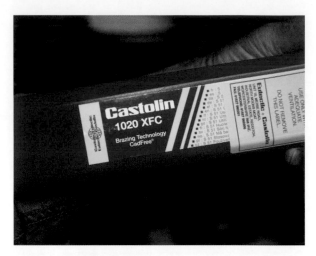

A good general purpose silver solder.

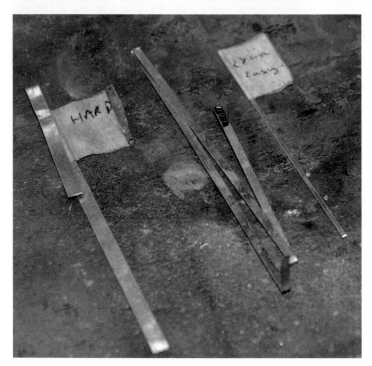

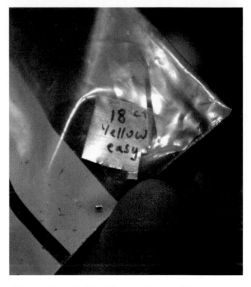

Above: 18ct Gold solder cut into paillons.

Left: Ribbons of jewellery-grade silver solders.

sizes which are aimed at professional use. Some industrial solders are easy to use across a wide range of applications, but will appear slightly yellow against sterling silver jewellery. The result is repairs that are obvious. Speak to your supplier with regard to colour when ordering any materials.

Flux

The traditional flux for silver solder work is borax, which would be in the form of a cone sitting in a coarse porcelain bowl. An amount of the crystals would be scraped into the bowl, mixed into paste with water and ground to the required consistency. Modern fluxes come as a paste, liquid or in some cases as a powder which contains an amount of silver. This 'solder paste' is mixed with water and is used primarily on fine cracks to promote penetration by capillary attraction.

A popular general purpose flux paste.

Pre-fluxed soldering rods are also available in a range of grades, some of which are prohibitively expensive, as they are only supplied in 500g packs. Your local DIY store may sell small quantities of pre-fluxed rod in a limited range of popular grades.

Some small local welding supply outlets will retail single rods when and if they are in stock. Welduk can supply a reasonable range of top quality solder in packs of five rods by mail order.

Work Surface

Traditionally asbestos mats were used to solder on, and indeed some textbooks on the subject have not yet been updated to say otherwise. You can also use a refractory brick. A simple safe alternative is to use a cuttlefish bone; these can be collected at no cost from any beach or can be bought from any pet shop. Cuttlefish bone has the advantage over both the asbestos mat and the refractory brick in that it is softer, and allows items to be pushed into the surface securely. It is also possible to cast small objects into hollows formed within the surface of cuttlefish bone using molten solder. Items which require heating and soldering from all sides are sat on a loose mop of wire, which is known as a 'jeweller wig'.

RISKS/SAFETY CONSIDERATIONS

● Nearly all of the materials used in silver soldering are toxic, some seriously, so you would need

A BEGINNER'S GUIDE TO SILVER SOLDERING

Stand the small object to be soldered on a refractory brick or heatproof table. Set up the work with the piece to be fixed in situ along with a small paillon of solder. This working field must be kept very clean, as any lead from previous soldering operations will denature any silver it comes into contact with, leaving it unworkable. For this reason it is standard practice to have more than one refractory brick, one of which is kept only for fine work.

Into the joint apply some wet flux – this might be done with a toothpick or similar fine applicator. Then heat the area with a blowtorch until the flux boils and the paillon of solder flows across and into the joint. If there are any gaps, use small slivers of silver to bridge them rather than the solder. Lay these in place and solder them in.
Be careful: overheating of the solder may result in some of the constituent metals parting company to leave permanent discolouration and a weak joint.

Once the solder has set, cool the workpiece by quenching it in clean water – this rapid cooling helps to loosen some of the fire-scale which is produced during the soldering process.

Remove any excess solder with a needle file and abrasive paper if required. Then clean the piece with a fine compound and polish to a brilliant shine with a proprietary metal polish and a soft cloth.

to consider extraction and possibly filtration to prevent any fumes being dumped into the surrounding environment. Likewise waste products will need to be disposed of carefully. This process involves naked flames and hot metal.
● Pressurized gases as used in a blowtorch demand careful storage and handling.
● A blowtorch which has a secure base and which can be operated with one hand will always be advantageous in this type of work.
● Check with your insurance company if you intend to work at home.

Bracelet repair. Bracelet has poor previous repairs using wrong solder.

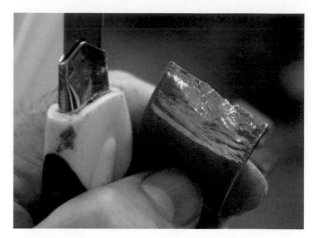

Old lead solder is thoroughly removed with blade.

Flux paste is mixed with water prior to application.

Hinge removed and flux applied.

Hinge set in place – flux and paillon applied.

Heat is carefully applied from blowtorch.

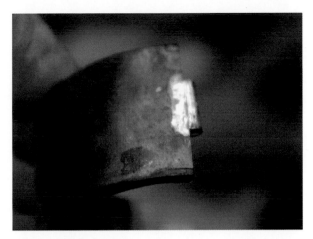

Solder has flowed nicely.

Other side of bracelet is repaired.

Work is quenched in cold water to loosen fire-scale.

Above and below: Fire-scale is polished off with compound.

Proprietary metal polish used to give final brilliant shine.

Detail shows applied strip and chasing work.

Detail of repair shows new solder to hinge.

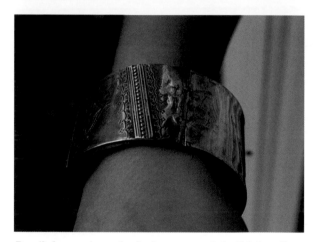

Detail shows mismatch of colour — repair is slightly yellow against original metal.

BRONZE REPAIRS

Repairs to bronze statuary are in essence the same as the silver solder exercise described here, but often involve much larger pieces which have to be securely held during the fixing process. Shown here is a small statue that has recently received a repair to one arm. As you can see the area around the site of repair is very different in colour to the rest of the piece. Much of the antique restorer's art is in 'patinating' the bronze with acids and metal salt solu-tions until the correct colour is achieved. The final finish will usually be with a wax.

Very large statuary may demand pre-heating in order to allow proper flow of the solder and to pre-vent it cooling too rapidly. It is often the case that one of the pieces to be joined will be considerably larger than the other. Care must be taken to ensure even heating of both sides of the joint, which may mean concentrating the flame on or pre-heating only the more massive piece.

Left: Bronze statuary is repaired using silver solder.

Above: This work often requires greater consideration regarding support.

Below: Consideration for unequal heat-soak.

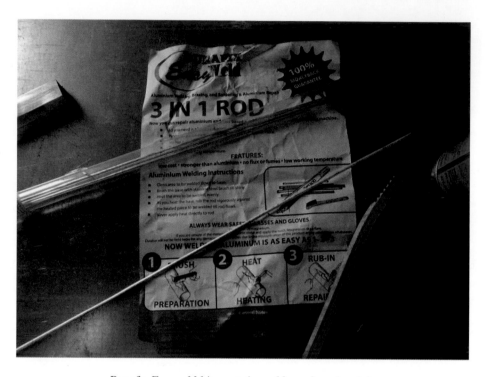

Durafix Easyweld kit comprises solder rods and stainless steel brush.

CHAPTER 5

Aluminium Brazing and Welding

Aluminium poses some problems for those wishing to join it. This is a very active metal which is regarded as 'self-anodizing' due to the thin layer of hard oxide which will be generated around the surface almost immediately after cleaning and when melted.

ALUMINIUM 'BRAZING'

In recent years a raft of products have come onto the market that claim to be able to 'weld' aluminium with nothing more than a blowtorch. A visit to any of the big classic car shows will see demonstrations of wonder welding wires, which seem to do the impossible before your eyes.

Strictly, some of these products should be termed as aluminium 'brazing', as true fusion is not necessarily achieved. One particular wire first solders and then welds when reheated. This material alloys itself with the parent metal during the second heating process and as such, does indeed weld the two pieces together. However, the material around the join will possess the properties of the new alloy and not of the original metal. This then raises the question of strength, which would need expert investigation to answer fully.

A trawl of the internet shows the consummate ease with which these processes are applied to the trickiest of jobs. After some investigation we have to say that these miracle products do actually work, but they are not as easy to use as the demonstrations would have you believe. With practice, though, anything is possible. This said, many well-respected companies endorse the use of these products.

Below is a selection of products for aluminium brazing. There are other products available; the selection described here are simply the ones which came to hand most readily. With all of these products, it will be found that a fair bit of practice is required to achieve anything like satisfactory results, despite what the demonstration videos will tell you.

Durafix Easyweld

Easyweld is a cheap and simple method of joining most grades of aluminium using only the heat from a butane blowtorch. Easyweld will adhere to copper and most non-ferrous metals (except stainless steel) and will join dissimilar metals. Zinc 'pot-metal' castings might also come within the range of material which can be joined with Easyweld – however, Zamac and Mazac castings specifically do not. This unfortunately means that it will be a matter of try it and see, as to which specific castings can and cannot be joined. This product can be successfully employed to repair castings and thin sheet items including alloy vehicle body panels. As such, it is offered as an alternative to Tig at a fraction of the cost, available in kits from around £15 from welduk.com. A full demonstration is available on the internet.

Before joining, clean the aluminium work pieces with a small stainless-steel wire brush, which is supplied in the kit, along with 5 sticks of welding rod. The brush effectively acts as a flux to strip away and break any oxides on the surface which would otherwise impede the flow of solder. When using the product to build up material along a join, use the rod itself to break the surface of the pool in order to allow it to flow. Use the blowtorch to heat the metal to 389°C (732°F), but not the alloy rod which would simply crumble.

When the joint area is evenly up to temperature, place the rod into it and watch as the solder flows onto the joint. Rubbing the joint with the rod will

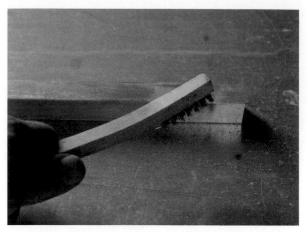

All surfaces to be joined must be cleaned with a wire brush, which acts as flux.

Pieces to be joined are set in place.

Joint is heated prior to addition of solder.

Rod is stroked against pre-heated joint to initiate flow of material.

DURAFIX EASYWELD

encourage it to flow, thus creating a greater build of new metal.

TechnoWeld

TechnoWeld is an apparently similar material, which comes in a kit with a stainless steel wire brush and steel abrader in the form of a fine rod. The brush is used to clean the weld area prior to welding and the abrader is used during the welding process, as a means of breaking the oxide layer which will form over the weld pool. Unlike Easyweld, this material can be used to repair and join Mazak and Zamak castings – which should be pre-heated in an oven to about 200°C before applying the rod in the usual way. TechnoWeld requires heating to 380°C (730°F). For more information go to techno-weld.co.uk on the internet.

Alutight

Alutight is a flexible wire which is supplied by the metre. If used properly, this amount of the material is capable of creating 30 metres of joint. The metal to be welded should be clean, but no special pre-treatment is needed. During heating to 380°C, stroke the joint area with an ordinary steel screwdriver, which breaks the surface of the oxide layer and allows the molten wire to flow along by capillary action. If you continue to heat the joint, the new material will alloy itself with the base metal to create a fused joint with full penetration. In practice, it is difficult to gauge when the metal has fused – a situation made worse when joining sections of different thickness. Alutight sells at a list price of £40, but you may be able to negotiate a more favourable price at a live demonstration.

RISKS/SAFETY CONSIDERATIONS

- Aluminium and its alloys are bright silver, as are all of the above products. A weak joint

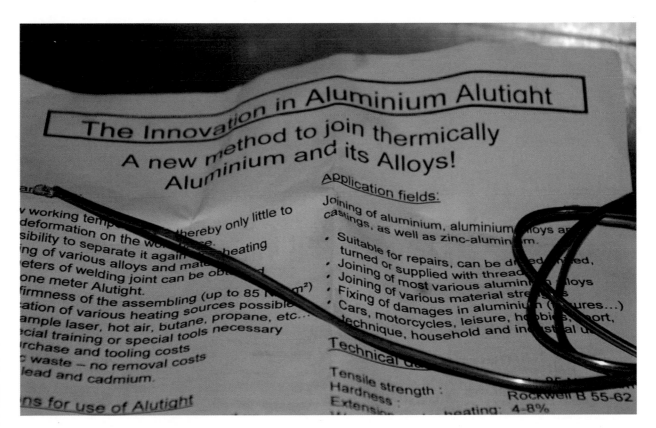

Alutight wire is available by the metre.

produced with any of these may well look exactly like a sound one. Destructive testing of practice pieces may be required to ensure confidence in any fabricated structure.

● Never use any of these products to repair alloy wheels or any safety-critical component.
● Do not attempt any of the above with an acetylene torch.
● Always wear safety glasses.
● Beware – aluminium may conduct heat further, and remain hot far longer than is expected.

ALUMINIUM WELDING

Traditional gas welding of aluminium is notoriously difficult, as the metal does not glow red in the same way as steel. As a result, anyone attempting to gas weld aluminium will find that it will melt without warning.

Mig welding of aluminium is possible with fairly low-powered equipment, though in practice the degree of skill needed will prove tricky for many. The weld pool is slow to establish, and once started must be moved along very quickly. As a rule you will require 25 per cent more power to initiate an aluminium weld with Mig compared to mild steel.

Tig welding of aluminium demands very expensive AC gear, which puts this process beyond the means of the hobbyist.

MMA stick welding of aluminium is also possible with the correct rod and a transformer-based welder.

Joint is set up and heated with torch before wire is touched to joint.

Material will run by capillary action along seam aided by stroking with screwdriver.

Joint is now soldered, but continued heating will cause new material to alloy.

Joint is now welded.

ALUTIGHT SOLDERING/WELDING WIRE

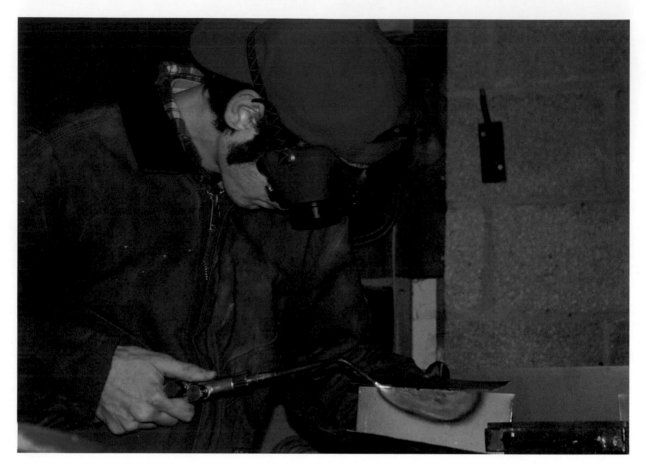

Gas welding in action.

CHAPTER 6

Oxy-acetylene Gas Welding and Brazing

Oxy-acetylene gas welding is a method of joining metal by use of a flame which is hot enough to heat a localized area to melting point so that two pieces can be fused. In the case of brazing the flame needs to be hot enough to melt a brass or bronze alloy rod to the point where it will bond with the surface of another metal.

WHAT METALS CAN IT JOIN?

It is commonly used to weld mild steel and with more difficulty, aluminium (and also to braze most common metals). Any metal or combination of metals which can be welded or brazed can be joined using gas welding – if the appropriate filler rod and flux are used.

WHAT IS IT USED FOR?

Gas was for many years the method of welding in vehicle repair. Gas welding is a traditional skill and for this reason alone will always have an appeal to those wishing to use the 'authentic' method. That aside, gas welding in the hands of an expert is a truly beautiful and elegant craft.

As a pure fusion means of joining sheet steel, it is well suited to the repair and fabrication of panel work and automotive work – especially 'hammer weld' techniques in which a short run of weld is performed before being dressed with a hammer and dolly. By this method the weld is brought up to shape, and some surface tension is imparted into the join. An experienced practitioner of hammer welding can join two halves of a panel almost

Welding kit complete with 'gas axe'.

Acetylene bottles contain gas dissolved in acetone which is in turn held in charcoal and cement.

Oxygen bottles contain gas at approximately 3000psi.

Welding bottles held on secure trolleys.

invisibly and without the need for fillers to bring the shape up to level prior to painting.

Though gas is the traditional method of welding in vehicle repair, it is limited, and therefore should not be selected as the only method of welding for the home vehicle restorer. It is more usual for a body shop to have to use gas welding in conjunction with Mig. More recently, Tig welding has been shown to offer many of the benefits of gas welding without its inherent drawbacks.

ALSO KNOWN AS?

Gas welding or OA welding.

HOW DOES IT WORK?

With both welding and brazing the flame is fuelled by oxy-acetylene gas, a mixture of oxygen and acetylene (to create a clean flame and high temperature). An alternative fuel for gas welding and brazing is oxy-mapp gas, a mixture of oxygen and mapp gas, which is a form of LPG (liquefied petroleum gas). Though more expensive than propane, it burns with a hotter flame.

The popular Turbo-Weld system uses disposable gas bottles and is a far cheaper alternative than oxy-acetylene, which involves more expensive gear and the additional cost of renting gas bottles. However, the price advantage is lost if more than occasional use is required. This equipment can be used for both soft and hard (silver) soldering and most other processes which demand direct heat, but due to the cost involved and very intense localized heat, you may find it preferable to use a blowtorch.

Rothenburger and Burnzomatic also sell mini gas sets, but call them brazing kits. In practice the oxy-mapp gas kit can be used to perform fusion welding or brazing, but you will find that learning to weld with this equipment will prove expensive, as the bottles have only a limited run time. When ordering a set you should invest in a second bottle of oxygen for each bottle of fuel. Very useful for applications such as the odd bit of bodywork or the fabrication of a pair of engine mounts, these kits are a handy addition to any workshop where other forms of welding are practised.

Oxygen
(AS PER A FULL-SIZED GAS WELDING SET)

Oxygen is held in bottles at a pressure of 200bar=3000psi and is released through a regulator at a safer working pressure via a rubber hose to the 'blowpipe' or torch. Acetylene, dissolved in acetone, is held in bottles at the much lower pressure of 15.5bar=240psi and is released through a regulator at a safe working pressure via a rubber hose to the blowpipe.

Oxygen bottles are usually black, but will definitely have a white shoulder colour. Acetylene is usually supplied in maroon bottles and will definitely have a maroon shoulder colour. Acetylene, due to its inherent instability, is contained in a mixture of cement and charcoal. It is essential that you become familiar with the proper handling and safety procedure for both of these gases and only keep them in a safe frame or trolley.

Regulators are attached by a brass gland seal and screw thread. Never use any form of lubrication on this equipment other than PTFE tape. Take care when fitting and do not use undue force or ill-fitting spanners. The acetylene regulator is threaded left-handed so as not to allow the wrong gear to be fitted. Any organic matter trapped in the valve of an oxygen bottle might spontaneously oxidize – with dramatic results.

Before the regulator is fitted, the cylinder must be cracked or snifted, which is to say, the valve is opened very briefly to blow out any debris. As gas is now supplied with a plastic cap over the valve, the likelihood of any foreign matter being present is low. Cracking the cylinder is alarmingly noisy, and as the pressure of the oxygen is so high you should always keep out of the line of fire and wear ear and eye protection. Traditional gas bottle keys are gradually being replaced with taps on the bottles, but it is a sound idea to keep at least one key in the workshop, as the supply of the newer bottles is inconsistent.

Once the regulator has been fitted, the gas valve must be opened and checked for leaks. Hissing or buzzing are good clues, as is sense of smell, if the gas in question has an odour. Acetylene has a distinct smell which you must become familiar with. Proprietary leak detector products are a good idea. Never use a lighted match to find a leak, and do not use soapy water on an oxygen cylinder or its attachments – the fat content may ignite.

Hoses are colour coded and generally long lived, but still need to be checked regularly for signs of scorching, perishing or cracking.

Blowpipe (torch)

The blowpipe (torch) is in three sections: the aluminium shank or main body, which features two gas control valves; the brass 'mixing chamber' in which the gases come together; and onto this is mounted the copper nozzle, which is matched to the flow of gas and in turn the size of flame required. Nozzles are numbered relative to their capacity. As such, a No.2 nozzle is designed to pass 2 cubic feet of gas per hour; this will also be numbered 57, which relates to cubic litres per hour.

The set-up described must also include a pair of flashback arrestors which, as the name implies, are devices which halt any flame which might otherwise

FLAME CONTROL

Igniting the flame should be with a spark-gun and never with a match or cigarette lighter, as a spark from the welding process could easily breach the matchbox or casing and lead to a flare-up or minor explosion.

With the regulators set and the torch pointed upward, the acetylene valve should be opened first, as oxygen alone cannot burn. Without oxygen however, acetylene will produce a sooty flame due to much of the gas not combusting efficiently.

The oxygen valve is then opened and the flame 'balanced'. As the oxygen is increased, you should see its cone, which is set to cover that of the acetylene. The hottest part of the flame is in the region of 3160°C (5720°F), which is at the tip of the inner light blue cone.

When lighting an oxy/fuel gas torch, always open the fuel gas valve first. Acetylene should be pointed upward and propane/mapp gas pointed downward.

Gas bottle valve and key.

Gas regulator has dial gauges for working pressure and bottle pressure.

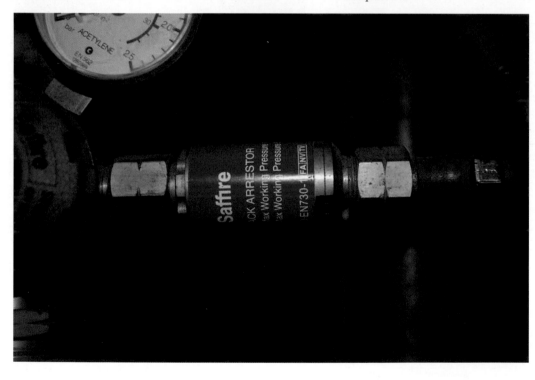

In line flashback arrestors are essential. This type is single use.

A BEGINNER'S GUIDE TO OXY-ACETYLENE WELDING

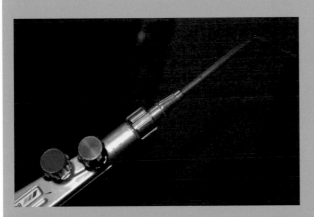

Blowpipe torch shows valves for acetylene (red) and oxygen (blue).

Start with your piece set up ready to weld and a clean No.1 or 2 nozzle on the torch, your goggles on your head, but not covering your eyes yet – and spark gun to hand.

Check that the gas controls on the torch are turned off, then turn the gas on at the bottles. Now making sure the tip is pointing away from you or anything that might get burnt, turn the gas dial up a little and strike your spark gun at the tip. A sooty yellow flame will shoot from the nozzle – the flame should be around 18–20cm (7–8in) long. Put down the spark gun and put your goggles on.

Slowly turn up the oxygen valve – too quickly and your flame will blow out. The flame should even out and become cone-shaped, with an outer blue cone of flame and an inner white cone, with a light blue cone in between. Be aware that the flame continues out further than what is visible. Adjust the oxygen using the cones as a guide to get the light blue and white cone to merge, becoming a rounded white cone about a centimetre long. This is called a neutral flame and is what you want for welding.

The hottest point of the flame is just in front of the white cone. Your aim is to heat both pieces evenly across the seam so as to melt them together. Aim the white cone at the seam approximately half a centimetre away from the piece and watch for colour changes in the metal – it should turn red then white. When the metal is white-hot it should be hot enough to join.

The flow of gas from the torch will act on the molten metal, so by moving the torch around you can effectively push the two white-hot edges of your piece together to fuse and form a weld. Move the flame along the seam in a small spiralling motion, or you can work from one side to the other to get even heating and fusion.

If your edges don't flow together use filler rod to bridge the gap – the filler rod will melt more quickly than the pieces and can be used to push the weld where you want it.

Be aware that when you first start your piece will be cold, so the time it takes to get your edges to the right temperature will be much longer than once the process is well underway.

Pay attention to flame and gas bottles. If your acetylene is running low your flame will become oxidizing, and while your metal can still look like it's welding, it's not really bonding – this join will be brittle and come apart easily.

Always pay attention to where exactly you are aiming the flame. Waving the torch around can easily lead to injury or damage. Playing the flame across the gas hoses is obviously dangerous. Consider getting a stand for the torch, and try not to practise alone. The value of another pair of hands and eyes is immeasurable.

The most common problem that will arise while learning gas weld is 'blowback' – this is a violent (but usually harmless) explosion within the tip of the torch. Blowback is caused by overheating the torch or too low a gas pressure. At most this 'pop' or 'crack' will

make you jump or will blow out the flame. Worse than this is when the blowback causes sparks to jump across the room, which poses a fire risk to any combustible material in the vicinity. More dangerous still is when the blowback occurs within the mixing chamber of the torch. If flashback arrestors are fitted you are never going to experience the worst-case scenario of an exploding bottle.

No.5 welding nozzle (number relates to gas flow in cubic feet).

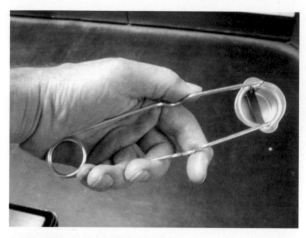

Spark gun used to safely ignite torch.

Sooty or carburizing flame caused by unburned fuel.

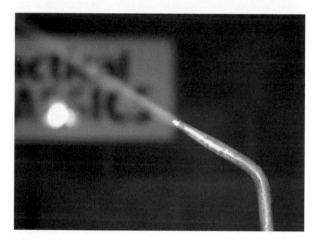

Neutral flame used for welding.

Oxidizing flame used for brazing, has too much oxygen.

creep back up the hose to the bottle. Better arrestors can be reset should they be triggered, where the cheaper ones are single use. In the event of a flash-back, the equipment should be carefully inspected to find the cause of the problem, and the acetylene bottle checked for hot-spots.

Balancing the Flame

When setting a flame for welding or brazing you should always aim for a balanced flame and then make any adjustment from there.

CARBURIZING OR SOOTY FLAME

If not enough oxygen is present in the flame, there will be unburned acetylene which will produce smoke which is generally unwanted. This flame can

be put to good use in the process of hard-facing – where carbon is added to the alloy – or to reduce the amount of oxide in a steel at the point of welding. It is also used to blacken aluminium prior to annealing. This flame is typified by a long yellow/white feather with a blue outer cone.

NEUTRAL OR BALANCED FLAME

This is the standard flame used to weld with, and is characterized by a neat light-blue cone surrounded by a second cone, which fades from dark blue to colourless.

The inner cone is where most of the acetylene is burned, while the outer is where hydrogen and carbon monoxide produced from acetylene burn on contact with atmospheric oxygen.

Above: Green flame cause by in-line fluxer.

Left: Oxy-acetylene set-up with in-line fluxer used for brazing work.

A BEGINNER'S GUIDE TO OXY-ACETYLENE GAS BRAZING

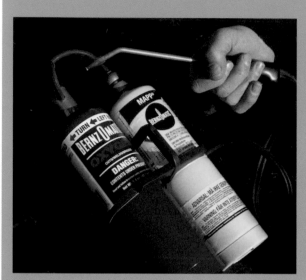

BurnzOMatic mini brazing kit.

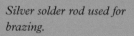

Silver solder rod used for brazing.

Brazing rods available from DIY shop.

Unlike oxyacetylene welding, with brazing you're not fusing the pieces to one another, but heating them and melting your filler rod onto them to create a joint. Unlike soldering, the rod itself needs to be heated to get it to melt.

It is standard practice before you start to take your filler rod and bend the end over with a pair of pliers so you don't accidentally poke yourself in the eye with it while you're working.

Mix up your flux and clean the edges of your pieces with a wire brush or emery paper. Brush your flux across the seam and set your pieces up ready to weld. (Pre-fluxed rods obviously should not require a separate flux, but don't be surprised if half of it has fallen off before you get to use it. A pot of general purpose flux is a useful addition to any workshop.)

Set 1 or 2 nozzle on the torch, your goggles on your head, but not covering your eyes yet, and spark gun to hand.

Check that the gas controls on the torch are turned off, then turn the gas on at the bottles. Now, making sure the tip is pointing away from you or anything that might get burnt, turn the gas dial up a little and strike your spark gun at the tip. A sooty yellow flame will shoot from the nozzle – your flame should be around 18–20cm (7–8in) long. Put down the spark gun and put your goggles on.

Slowly turn up the oxygen valve – too quickly and your flame will blow out. The flame should even out and become cone-shaped with an outer blue cone of flame and inner white cone and a light blue cone in between. Be aware that the flame continues out further than is visible. Adjust the oxygen using the cones as a guide to get the light blue and white cone to merge becoming a rounded white cone about a centimetre long. This is called a neutral flame and is hot enough to melt your pieces together, but for brazing you only want to heat your pieces to red-hot, so we will add more oxygen to give an oxidizing flame.

Start by waving the flame across your seam just to make the flux flow. (For those using a pre-fluxed rod go straight to the next step.)

Next take your filler rod and hold it near your seam. Move the torch in so that the cone of the flame is approximately 1cm away from the piece and move it back and forth from one side of the joint to the other until the metal starts to turn red. Now bring the filler rod

Stepped lap joint set-up.

Joint is heated prior to introduction of rod.

Braze is 'flowed' into joint.

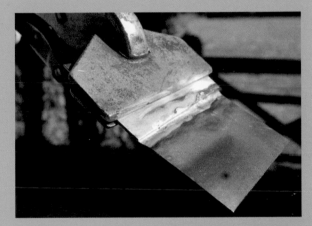

Finished joint shows brazing.

FORMING A CAPILLARY BRAZE JOINT

in to touch the seam, and direct your flame at the tip of the rod. The filler rod will conduct the heat much better than the piece, so shouldn't need to be heated for as long – your aim here is to heat the rod while still keeping the seam red-hot.

Your filler rod should melt and flow into the hot seam. Move the rod and flame along the seam to draw the established braze along the join. Try to ensure that you are heating both sides of the join equally, as the liquid braze is attracted to the heat and so will tend to only stick to the hotter side, if one side is hotter.

If your braze runs or drips away from your seam, your metal is not hot enough. If you overheat the braze, the metals will separate and the joint will be inferior. This is apparent through a discoloration in the brazing, particularly patches of red from the copper separating.

If you go back over your brazed joint and reinforce it with further build-up of braze, melting the rod onto what has already been put on, you now have what is known as 'braze welding'. The same process is used for bronze welding, but using a bronze rod, which melts at a higher temperature.

In common with gas welding the most common problem that you will encounter is 'blowback', usually a loud 'pop' or 'crack' caused by the gas igniting within the tip of the torch. This can be avoided by turning up the gas pressure or backing the torch off a tad.

Metal is heated prior to addition of braze.

Braze rod is flowed into hole in top layer of metal.

A slighty messy – though sound – stud braze alongside a Mig stud.

FORMING A BRAZE STUD

OXIDIZING FLAME

Typified as being white and rather fierce; it often has a purplish inner cone. The oxidizing flame is used commonly in brazing. As the name suggests, it is rich in oxygen and will actively add this to the weld, so may demand a more aggressive flux. This flame can actually burn hotter than the neutral flame, but as the heat is more evenly distributed, it is softer in use.

OXY-ACETYLENE BRAZING

As we have discussed, brazing is the usual term for making a joint by using a brass-based alloy rod, in which the brass is 'flowed' by capillary action into joint. Brass welding is a similar process, but differs in as much as the rod is melted directly onto the joint to form a shoulder or reinforcement. Bronze welding is essentially the same again, but employs a bronze-based rod (*see* Chapter 1). The term braze

Joint is preheated before addition of braze rod.

A blob of braze – continued heating would cause this to flow.

Additional brass is added as a shoulder of material.

Brass welding. This is a very strong method of jointing.

BRASS WELDING

implies the use of brass as a filler or bonding material, and indeed brass and bronze are widely used for this purpose. However, 'brazing' might also refer to the use of a flame torch or brazier. Thus aluminium 'brazing' involves a blowtorch and a silver-coloured aluminium alloy wire (*see* Chapter 5).

RISKS/SAFETY CONSIDERATIONS

● Explosive gases stored in heavy bottles demand careful storage and handling.
● Invest in a decent set of flashback arrestors, but do not assume if one trips out there is not a problem.
● Failure to rectify a fault may lead to disaster. Check acetylene bottles for hot-spots, and in the event of a fire you must remove any bottles

Example of brazed joint on engine block.

Pre-fluxed brazing rod.

at risk to a safe distance of 200 metres away from any buildings.

- Allowing the flame to play over gas hoses poses a risk of fire or explosion.
- Sparks from welding or 'blowback' can ignite combustible materials away from the site of weld. Cigarette lighters and matches should not be permitted within the workshop for this reason.
- When in use, the welding flame is invisible along much of its length.
- This process produces hot metal items which may cool more slowly than is imagined.
- Many metals will produce toxic fumes when welded. Zinc will cause metal fume fever, while alloy additives such as beryllium are very toxic and may produce far worse illness.

- A torch stand will lessen problems caused by having to put down the torch whilst working. Hoses pose a tripping hazard.
- Many fume/gas combinations are heavier than air – which must be considered when working in a cellar, pit or other closed environment.
- It is essential that you become familiar with the correct procedure for the gases you are using, and that you notify anyone else nearby as to what you have on your premises. BOC will provide all the relevant safety and handling information.
- In the event of an emergency, clarification is essential. Warning stickers are available for your workshop and any vehicle used to transport pressurized gas.

A row of perfect welds – no further finishing is required.

CHAPTER 7

Resistance Spot Welding

Resistance spot welding is a method of joining (most commonly) sheet metal by use of an electrical current which is passed between two copper electrodes. During the welding process, and for some 'cooling time' immediately after, the electrodes apply a pressure which results in the finished weld being approximately the same thickness as one of the two sheets which have been fused.

WHAT METALS CAN IT JOIN?

For our purposes resistance spot welding can be used to join mild steel, galvanized steel, and some grades of 'semi-stainless' (or bright) steel. In industrial use, other metals such as aluminium can be spot welded, for example Land Rover bodywork.

WHAT IS IT USED FOR?

Resistance spot welding has many advantages over other forms of welding, especially in the area of vehicle repair and restoration, as this was the method employed during manufacture, and produces little or no heat distortion. The process is quick, demands no real skill and requires little or no cleaning up of the weld area afterwards. However, it is not realistically possible to employ only resistance spot welding, and so another method of welding will have to be used alongside it. The combination of spot welder and Mig is probably the ideal for body shop use.

This process was discovered accidentally in the 1930s and was soon put to good use in the aircraft and motor-vehicle manufacturing industries. Resistance spot welding quickly established itself as the norm in vehicle mass production. These days robotic and multi-electrode welders have to a great extent replaced manual spot welding on the production line, though the hand-operated machine has always had a place in the repair body shop. Spot welding has been largely overlooked by the home restorer in favour of gas and Mig.

The limitations of this form of welding are due to the need for an overlap and access to both sides of the joint. Vehicles which have been assembled using this form of welding have been put together in a specific build order. When repairing or restoring the same car, it will be found that no access can be gained to many of the seams and so an alternative method of welding will have to be found. A good example of this is the Triumph Stag – which had both front wings, the front deck and front lower valance made up as a sub-assembly which was pulled backward over the front of the car and welded onto the flitch plates and A-posts. Consequently it is impossible to replicate the joints between the front of the front wings where they meet with the front deck or valance. Close attention to the original build order can allow great savings in time and hassle when rebuilding vehicles such as the Mini or Triumph Spitfire. Clever use of the spot welder will justify your financial investment many times over.

Single-sided spot welders became available through the 1990s and rely on the use of two alternating earth leads. The single-sided welder would be a boon to any home restorer, but for the huge cost of this equipment. Shown on page 70 is a state of the art water-cooled inverter spot machine which is both single-sided and with a pincer. This machine currently retails for a whopping £7.5k + VAT.

ALSO KNOWN AS?

Spot welding or electrical welding.

Nut used to adjust closing point and pressure of electrodes.

Spotmatic has built-in timer.

Spotmatic machine shows adjuster.

HOW DOES IT WORK?

The most common form of spot welder is a one-piece unit consisting of a transformer, a handle/trigger and a pair of arms, onto which a pair of matched electrodes is mounted. This basic machine relies on the operator to squeeze the handle/trigger assembly to switch the current on and then pull it further until the power is cut again. In this way the pressure is still applied after the current has stopped, which allows the weld to cool without breaking.

More sophisticated models will feature a timer which might be inbuilt or sited in a separate box. The latest machines have digital controls, which account for time and metal thickness to calculate the optimum weld time – these can be overruled and compensated for by the operator.

A huge range of electrode/arm combinations can be found, but most machines will come with only the basic short set shown here.

BUYING A RESISTANCE SPOT WELDER

It is possible to buy a basic spot welder from one of the specialist restoration companies such as Frost. One alternative is to purchase a used machine from a professional body shop which has been upgraded to a more sophisticated unit. The Sealey machine featured on page 68 was acquired in this way and then returned to the manufacturer for a service.

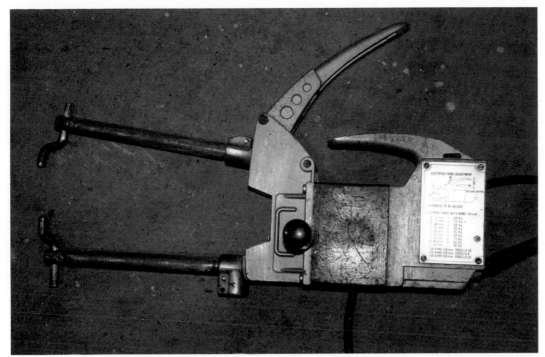

Spotmatic welder shown with longer arms for mid panel work.

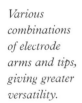

Various combinations of electrode arms and tips, giving greater versatility.

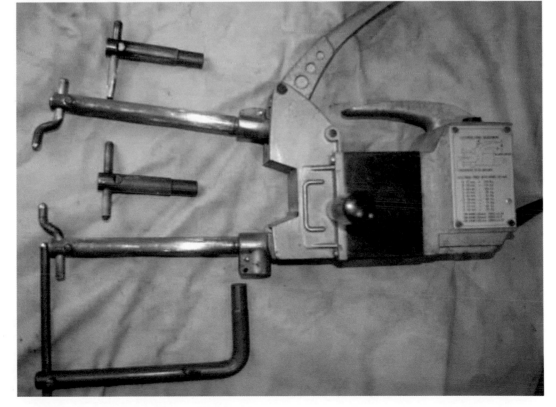

A BEGINNER'S GUIDE TO THE SPOT WELDER

Left: Sealey spot welder was all but ubiquitous in body shop trade.
Above: Standard electrode tip must be kept in good shape.

This old Sealey spot weld gun was common to many body shops for many years. It usually only requires the power lead to be uncoiled before it is ready for use.

A quick check of the state of the electrodes is a good idea, to make sure they have good round tips which meet evenly. By squeezing the trigger before the thing is turned on, we can gauge the pressure and if need be, place a single thickness of metal between the tips and adjust the turnbuckle until the gap is correct. Should you need to change the electrode arms or tips, you will need to set the position at which the points close by this same method.

Ideally, you will clamp the work securely after removing all paint and grease from the area to be joined. Contamination not only hinders the weld but can also pose a fire risk.

Uncoil the cable to prevent it overheating and ensure any extension lead is able to cope with the load. Turn the power on and wear safety glasses, as there is a risk of spitting.

Adopt a well-balanced stance, as the spot welder is quite heavy and gets heavier as the job progresses – especially if you have to use it overhead or at arm's length.

Set the machine so that the work is between the tips, and then close them until it is gripped. Now as you pull the trigger, you will feel the switch engage and hear the power coming in. A typical weld takes about a second and you will very soon get a feel for a 'good weld', which is one that holds without overheating.

When the weld is formed, you squeeze a bit tighter and the machine will give a 'clunk', which means that the power has been cut. Hold it like this for a second or two so as to allow the weld to cool. If you were to release the electrodes too early, there is a good chance that the two parts would spring apart, as the hot metal has no tensile strength. Poorly formed welds will fail with a 'crack', but usually respond well to being re-welded. A good weld needs virtually no cleaning up and looks original.

Alternative tip shapes.

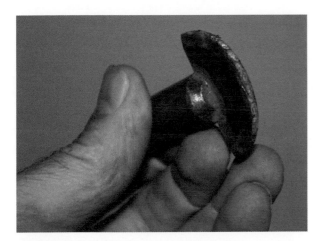

Half-round tip used to create roof seams.

Drill-mounted tool used to dress electrode tip.

WELDING EXAMPLE						
THICKNESS mm.	TIME	B	FORCE	D	ARMS mm.	SPOT/hour
0.8+0.8	0.15"	4 mm.	80 Kg.	58mm.	125	380
1+1	0.35"	4,5mm.	90 Kg.	65mm.	125	280
1,5+1,5	0.8"	5 mm.	100 Kg.	68mm.	125	120
2+2	1,25"	6 mm.	120 Kg.	72mm.	125	60
0.8+0.8	0.2"	4 mm.	50 Kg.	62 mm.	250	400
1,5+1,5	1.2"	5 mm.	65 Kg.	68mm.	250	120
1+1	0,6"	4,5mm.	45 Kg.	70mm.	350	300
1+1	1"	4,5mm.	36 Kg.	70mm.	500	300

SPOTMATIC

F CLASS   ITEM M

Forming a spot weld – pressure is applied through electrodes during welding.

Guidelines on machine for set-up.

Spot welder is ideal for forming boxwork.

Destructive testing used to determine quality of weld.

Expect to pay a couple of hundred pounds for a used machine or a basic unit. Current Sealey machines run out at approx £600 for the more modest machine and nearer £900 for the fuzzy logic controlled unit.

It is a good idea to invest in a tool to dress the tip of the electrodes as they will become deformed with continued use. Shown on page 69 is a drill-mounted dressing tool.

RISKS / SAFETY CONSIDERATIONS

● The electric spot welder is a heavy and cumbersome machine which is mains-operated and has a trailing power cable. In use, the item will very soon feel a lot heavier than is originally believed. Use of the device overhead or at arm's length demands good balance and a fair amount of physical strength.

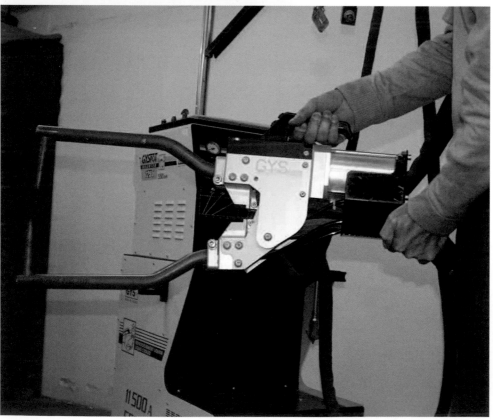

Above: Single-sided spot welder would be a restorer's dream, but for cost.

Left: Top of the range water-cooled welder.

● A wet vehicle or workshop brings a risk of electric shock, as does careless handling. A puddle and a gold wedding band can provide a quick route to earth for the power from this machine.

● When working on a vehicle, it is recommended that the battery be disconnected or a surge protector fitted across its terminals.

● Always wear eye protection, as some spitting of sparks from the weld is normal.

Above: Earth lead on pro machine is bolted or clamped to work.

Above: Pillar has concealed Mig joint, revealing limitations of spot welder.

Left: New panel is fixed with spot welder.

Welding torch and stick electrode rod.

CHAPTER 8

MMA or Stick Welding

MMA (manual metal arc) welding is electrical arc welding at its most primitive. A transformer or inverter delivers current to a torch (pos+), which holds a consumable electrode that is coated with flux. If the tip of the electrode is held in close proximity to the earthed (neg–) workpiece, then an arc will be generated between them that allows material from the electrode to be melted onto the workpiece.

WHAT METALS CAN IT JOIN?

So far as we are concerned, MMA can be used to join mild or stainless steel. It is not well suited to light sheet metal work or automotive applications. Some may find this method useful for the repair of cast-iron work. With the correct electrodes, MMA can be employed to join copper and aluminium, though the latter may require an AC-equipped machine.

WHAT IS IT USED FOR?

Anyone wishing to mend or fabricate garden gates and railings, or maybe plant and farm equipment, should consider the MMA process; though many would say that Mig has for the most part taken over in these areas. Stick welding is fairly easy to master and can be used to join and repair pretty heavy gauges of steel. The advantage of MMA in open-air situations is that Mig is prone to having the shielding gas blown away, where MMA does not. In use MMA does produce appreciable amounts of smoke, which must be safely removed from the work area. Older-type transformer units are considerably cheaper to buy than their modern inverter counterparts, and are less prone to problems

caused by unstable voltage. Thus, the older-type machines are more suited to site work or use with a generator. When compared amp for amp, an inverter may cost three times as much as an older-type transformer welder.

ALSO KNOWN AS?

● Stick welding refers to the stick of flux-coated metal, which is the electrode.
● Arc welding, which is accurate but not very specific, as the name came into use before Mig and Tig became familiar.
● Electric welding – again not very specific.
● Shielded arc welding is common in America, but is misleading as no separate shielding gas is used in the process; any gas present is generated by the flux in the arc itself.

We will use either MMA or stick from here on.

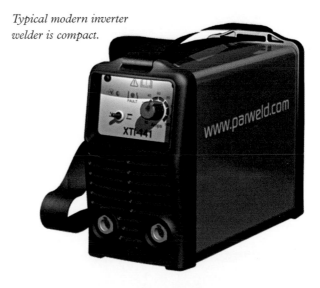

Typical modern inverter welder is compact.

Typical control panel of modern inverter welder.

'Dinse' plug connectors for torch and earth lead.

HOW DOES IT WORK?

The transformer or inverter has two leads coming out of it: one is the 'live' and the other the 'return' which is commonly referred to as the 'earth'. To the live we attach an electrode – this is coated in a flux and is consumed during the process as the flux burns away and the core of steel is deposited on the site of weld.

After the arc is struck, it must be maintained by keeping the electrode at a constant distance from the workpiece as the electrode erodes. Obviously, if the electrode contacts the base metal, the arc will collapse and a great deal of heat will build at the site of contact. Should the electrode be moved too far away, the arc will grow weak and ultimately fail. Other factors which will affect the arc and its ability to weld are: the current, the diameter of the electrode, the quality of earth, and the speed at which the electrode is moved. Less obvious is the angle of the electrode relative to the workpiece, which will have an effect on the electrode's ability to transfer material.

Older transformer machines, though cheaper than the newer inverter units, are much larger when like-for-like outputs are compared. Control for the MMA welder is basically a matter of selecting the correct output power for the job.

Electrodes

The stick electrode is a metal rod with a concentric coating of flux which is often tapered at one end to aid striking of the arc, and is sometimes given a graphite coating. The other end of the stick has no coating, so as to allow contact with the live torch.

MMA stick electrodes are supplied in varieties of core material and coating as well as thickness to exactly suit a job. You must match the core of the electrode to the base material which you are welding. Some types of stainless steel can be used to join carbon steel to itself or join carbon steel to stainless steel; more exotic core materials such as aluminium

ELECTRODE THICKNESS MATCHED TO AMPERAGE

[BS] Electrode diameter (mm)	[BS] Current (Amps min/max)
1.6	25–50
2	40–70
2.5	60–110
3.25	100–140
4	140–180
5	180–200A

This guide is for carbon (mild) steel, and should be adhered to in order to achieve good penetration. A 5mm stick will produce a bead of material comparable to three passes from a 2.5mm stick.

A BEGINNER'S GUIDE TO MMA WELDING

Arc welding is probably the least sophisticated of all welding and for that reason is the easiest to do – and possibly the hardest to master.

Begin with your pieces clean and set up for welding. Clamp on your earth, clamp a fresh electrode into the holder and prepare to have very little idea what your weld pool is actually doing. Because of the flux coating on the electrode the welding arc produces a lot of smoke, sparks and slag material, all of which make it very hard to see your weld pool at all.

Start by switching on your machine, setting it to just below the highest power setting for the size of rod you are using. With your welding visor on, hold the stick at around 45 degrees to the piece. Establish an arc by touching the tip of the electrode to metal, then breaking contact with it and raising the tip to just

above the metal until you see an electrical arc jump from the tip of the rod to the metal. Typically you want an arc of around half a centimetre, but you'll need to control this by feeding the rod into the arc as it burns away. Watch the arc closely and try to keep it controlled and steady. Establishing and maintaining a good arc is the key to this type of welding.

Now try to create a line of weld by drawing the stick along your seam, feeding the stick into the weld pool as you go. Herein lies the difficulty: because the flux on the stick melts over the weld, sealing it from oxidization as you go, you can't work back over the weld you've just done – because the flux is no longer fluid. So do lots of practice where the result doesn't really matter.

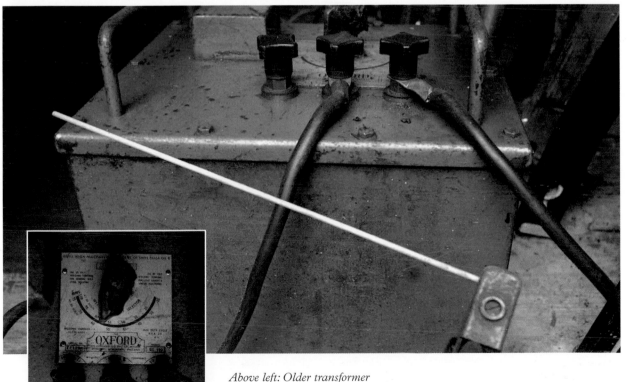

Above left: Older transformer welder is heavy and cumbersome.

Left: Current control on older machine.

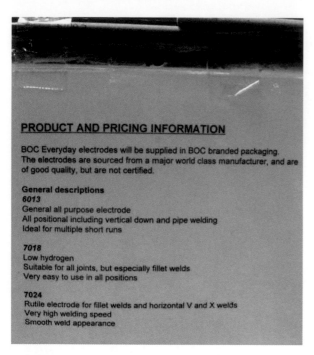

PRODUCT AND PRICING INFORMATION

BOC Everyday electrodes will be supplied in BOC branded packaging.
The electrodes are sourced from a major world class manufacturer, and are
of good quality, but are not certified.

General descriptions
6013
General all purpose electrode
All positional including vertical down and pipe welding
Ideal for multiple short runs

7018
Low hydrogen
Suitable for all joints, but especially fillet welds
Very easy to use in all positions

7024
Rutile electrode for fillet welds and horizontal V and X welds
Very high welding speed
Smooth weld appearance

Stick electrodes at point of sale – BOC 6013 is standard for most jobs.

will require an AC-equipped machine. It may also be found that some electrodes will require DC – and the use of such materials with any particular machine will have to be taken up with your supplier.

Coatings

Electrode coatings are referred to by their major constituent: basic or low-hydrogen electrodes are slightly less easy to use and can produce a rougher weld with more slag when compared to rutile electrodes, but the inherently lower hydrogen levels means a stronger weld with less chance of cracking. Rutile or GP (general purpose) electrodes contain rutile-sand, a form of titanium, so they give easy use across a wide range of applications with minimal slag and they leave a smooth attractive look to the weld; however, a property of this type is the production of hydrogen, which can leave the weld brittle when compared to other types. Cellulosic coatings contain cellulose, an organic material high in hydrogen; they are used for deep penetration and vertically downward applications; they produce rough welds with a fair amount of spatter. Duel coat sticks, as the name suggests, have the best properties of each and can be used over a wide range of applications including poorly prepared joints.

Melting/Hardening Speed

The other factor when selecting an electrode is its characteristics with regard to speed of melting and hardening – sometimes referred to as 'fill' and 'freeze': fast fill (quick to melt, fast freeze (quick to harden) and fill freeze or fast follow (intermed-

A range of electrode rods available from high street motoring shop.

Preparing to weld – electrode is live.

iate qualities). These terms are commonly used in America and to a lesser extent in Britain.

The rate at which an electrode melts will govern the speed at which you can work, while its hardening rate will have a bearing on which applications it is best suited to. Attempting to weld overhead with a material such as molten metal, which cannot defy gravity, is always a concern. The exact position of a run of weld may dictate which electrode you select. For example, some will work in any position except directly downward.

That said, it may well be that a 2.5mm basic stick is all you will ever need. For illustration and demonstration purposes we have used a BOC 6013 basic low hydrogen rod. At 40/50 amps it will join 20swg steel sheet without burning and can be employed across a wide range of applications.

Slag

Slag is unwanted dross created during the welding process. More than any other form of welding, the MMA process is associated with slag. The process relies upon the electrode's coating to burn off in the arc to produce a shielding gas and flux. MMA is less efficient than Mig in transferring material, so much of the bulk of each stick is either vaporized or deposited as slag on the weld surface. If you are not careful, this slag can interfere with the bonding process or successive passes of weld. In a typical case, you might be joining two pieces of plate with a root run on each, and slag might cause a failure of the two runs or successive runs to fuse. Or slag may interfere with the fusion of two parts or become entrapped behind a section of the joint. This can be dangerous as slag which contains flux can encourage corrosion in time. A wire brush and a chipping hammer will usually be supplied with your welder, and their use must be considered as an essential part of the process.

CAST-IRON REPAIRS

Cast-iron cored electrodes are available, but it is worth considering the use of pure nickel to repair cast-iron work such as engine blocks or machinery. Depending on the age of the piece in question,

Tip of electrode is scratched against work to initiate arc.

much of what is regarded as 'iron' will in fact be made of steel. The original definition of steel which is produced from iron was based upon the carbon content. Iron in a pure state would be too soft for most of our purposes.

There are two approaches to the repair of cast-iron with MMA: cold arc or pre-heat. In cold arc welding, short stitches (2–4cm) are applied and allowed to cool to hand-hot before continuing. The work is done with as low a current as possible, and each run of weld is hammered immediately after it is laid down. The fracture to be repaired must be completely free of oil and grease and should be prepared with a grinder to allow good penetration and build. In this process, no pre-heating of the work is used. One advantage of this method is that less stripping is require when working on machinery.

Pre-heating and controlled cooling are employed to allow greater penetration of the weld and to counter the chances of cracking as the weld cools (*see* Chapter 13).

Buttering and studding are also useful when dealing with cast-iron (*see* Chapter 1).

Electrode is lifted and arc is in force.

Typical first attempt at MMA welding – sound if not pretty.

RISKS/SAFETY CONSIDERATIONS

- Heavy flameproof overalls are a must, as is a good quality mask. Consider getting leather aprons, sleeves, hats and gauntlets. Buy a welding helmet of the correct shade – self-darkening masks will improve your ability no end.
- The MMA welder is a heavy and cumbersome machine, though the newer inverter units are considerable smaller and lighter than the older type.
- The process is mains-powered and produces an electrical arc and a lot of white-hot spatter.
- All welding processes involve hot metal, which may take a long time to cool.
- Fumes from welding are toxic and may be heavier than air.
- Additives used in the production of welding electrodes include many exotic and highly poisonous metals such as beryllium.
- Radiation from this process may cause burns or irritation.
- MMA produces gaseous ozone, which is known to cause delayed lung damage.
- Health problems associated with these chemicals may not make themselves known for some time.
- Never underestimate the need for proper extraction and ventilation.

Gasless Mig produces some spatter.

CHAPTER 9

Mig Welding

Mig (metal inert gas) welding is a form of electrical arc welding which is shielded from oxidizing by an inert gas; this is usually taken to be argon, but as we shall see later can be a combination of gases, some of which are not strictly inert.

WHAT METALS CAN IT JOIN?

Mild steel, aluminium and stainless steels can be welded if the appropriate wire/gas combinations are used. Mig braze allows a greater range of metals to be joined. Aluminium welding demands approximately 25 per cent more power than steel, and this must be accounted for when choosing a welder.

WHAT IS IT USED FOR?

The Mig welder is the ideal choice for any enthusiast wishing get involved in car repair/restoration or fabrication work. Smaller machines of up to about 150 amps are capable of welding steel sheet from 0.8mm to about 2mm in a single pass. Greater thickness will require several passes of the torch or a heavier-duty machine. Buy a welder rated at between 100 and 200 amps. Gasless Mig should be considered if a lot of outdoor work is planned.

Easier to master than both Tig and gas welding, the Mig has come to dominate welding in the commercial body shop and fabrication industry. In its simplest form, Mig welding can be applied within seconds of setting up the machine. Rudimentary spot welds (strictly called stud welds) which are used to affix vehicle panels, do not require any previous experience or practice.

For the benefit of the small-time consumer, both wire and gas can be purchased in moderate amounts at low cost. Disposable cylinders of CO_2 for steel and pure argon for aluminium welding are available. Refillable small CO_2 cylinders are also to be found at Sealey stockists. These remove the need to rent a full-sized cylinder from a gas supplier. Gasless Mig wire also negates the need to buy gas, but the relatively high cost per metre may outweigh the initial benefit, beyond some level of use.

ALSO KNOWN AS?

- Mag (metal active gas) welding is the same process when CO_2 is the shielding gas.
- Shielded arc welding covers both Mig and Mag; unfortunately this term is also applied to Tig welding and MMA.
- Argon arc welding is self-explanatory, but again is also applied to Tig.
- GSMA (gas shielded metal arc) welding is quite a mouthful, but is strictly accurate and all encompassing; this term is commonly used in America.
- Sigma (shielded inert gas metal arc) welding is an early term that has largely been consigned to history.
- Gasless Mig (also known as flux-cored arc welding or FCAW) welders work on the same principles but have a 'flux-cored' wire – that is, the wire itself contains the shielding gas. In this process the electrical polarity is reversed, so that the work is live and the torch earthed. Good for outdoor and on-site work (see below). Gas/no-gas machines are available.

Mig brazing is a relatively new development which allows us to join the new high-tensile steel alloys which have come into use in vehicle manufacture. Mig brazing also gives us the option for joining

0.7kg reel of Mig welding wire.

Typical controls on 130 amp machine.

Wire transport system.

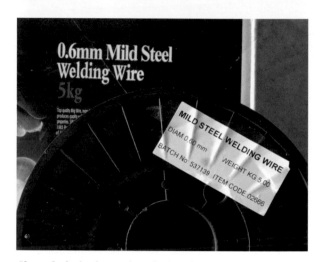

5kg reel of wire for semi-professional work.

Torch internals.

some dissimilar metals. Please note that this process is currently only possible with top-of-the-range machines and for now is perhaps not applicable to the amateur.

We will stick to the term Mig from now on. The name is common parlance in Britain and will be used to cover both Mig and Mag welding – that is, use of the Mig welder regardless of which gas is in use.

HOW DOES IT WORK?

(AS PER WELDING MILD STEEL)

The Mig welder is essentially a transformer and a wire transport system, along with a bottle of gas. The spool of copper-coated mild steel wire is fed via a motorized capstan through a liner up to the tip of the torch. When the trigger is depressed, the tip of the torch is made live; simultaneously the gas valve is opened and the wire transport system activated. Consequently, as the wire touches the workpiece – which is earthed – contact is made and an arc is formed. This in turn transfers metal from the wire onto the work. So if we can balance the rate of feed of wire from its spool to the rate at which it is melted, we are able to produce a continuous deposition of new metal. The immediate area in which the weld occurs is purged of oxygen by an inert gas which also issues from the torch.

Controls for wire speed and amperage are situated on the machine, and the gas is regulated from the bottleneck. More sophisticated machines include a solenoid to control the gas flow, while the simpler will have a sprung valve which is depressed

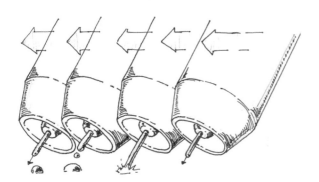

MIG welding transfer.

CO_2/ARGON

CO_2 was originally used as the shielding gas in Mig welding, but many found this to be too cold. CO_2/argon mixes are commonly used today, the proportions of which are matched to particular jobs. A universal grade is available. Pure CO_2 is used to lift beer in pubs, and this can at a push be successfully used to weld mild steel; it is considerably cheaper than the 'proper' argon/CO_2 mixtures.

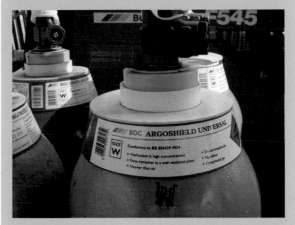

Argon/CO_2 shielding gas in bottle with regulator.

manually at the trigger. Copper-coated steel wire is commonly found in 0.6 and 0.8mm for light work and 1mm and 1.2mm for heavier industrial applications. Wire size must be matched to the transport system and amperage range of the particular machine. The welder's earth lead must be clamped to the workpiece – either directly or indirectly (via a steel bench), as a sound electrical connection is essential to good welding.

Welding Power Source

Known as the transformer, this is more correctly a welding rectifier. A critical part of the power source is of course a transformer which drops the mains AC voltage to a more usable DC current. The quality of the transformer construction will govern its longevity and ability to deliver prolonged service. The material from which the transformer is made

POWER RATING

Stable power is more important than big power. Most welders are used for the vast majority of the time at their lower output settings. Select a welder with an output to match its intended job. The number given in the name is often optimistic.

Welders which are rated at above about 150 amps are not designed to be run from the domestic 13 amp supply, so a machine of 180 amps might be restricted to its lower ranges. Remember that a 180 amp welder running at 150 amps will perform better than a 150 amp machine running flat out.

will also have an impact on the machine's overall weight.

The power controls on the front panel will relate to output amperage. Voltage is taken care of by the machine and is not a concern for our purposes. On higher output machines the voltage will govern the exact way in which the metal is transferred across the arc.

Costlier and more sophisticated machines will usually feature a rotary control to select output power while cheaper units will tend to have two or three rocker switches.

Wire Transport System

Domestic machines will be designed to accept wire spools of 0.7kg and 5kg; these will be of 0.6 and 0.8 mm diameter. The spool is usually mounted so that the wire feeds from the bottom in order to maintain the correct tension and not unravel. From the spool, the wire is fed into the 'rolls', which consist of a grooved capstan (which is usually mounted directly onto a motor) and a pinch-wheel. The pinch-wheel is set in such a way as to be quick-released and with an adjustable pressure. From the rolls, the wire is fed into a plastic liner which continues up a welding lead to the torch. The wire speed is controlled by a dial on the front panel of the unit. More upmarket machines will also have a control for 'burn-back', which adjusts the wire after each weld to give the correct length beyond the electrode tip.

Steel welding wire is given a coat of copper to protect it and to aid electrical conduction. Poorly stored wire will gain a fine encrusting of rust. Do not use wire with any trace of corrosion, as it will only foul the liner and lead to wire jam. Expect to pay in the region of £16 for a 5kg reel of welding wire.

The Torch

The welding lead and torch can be considered together to some extent. The lead is generally made up of a polythene sheath which contains the gas pipe, power lead, wire liner and the control wire for the power supply. Professional machines will come with a euro-connector which allows the lead/torch assembly to be unplugged from the main body of the machine to facilitate easy replacement.

The torch head contains switches for both the gas and the welding current, which are triggered simultaneously. Most of the welders in our price bracket will have manual brass gas valves, whereas more expensive units might feature an electrical switch, which would control a remote solenoid in the main body of the machine. The end of the torch features a copper tip through which the wire passes and is made live. Around the tip is the shroud which helps to direct the gas. Pronged shrouds are available for creating stud welds; the prongs allow the torch to be rested on the work while the joint is made.

Both tips and shrouds are considered to be consumables and are best replaced regularly to ensure consistent welding. Tips will wear as the wire passes through the central hole, which leads to poor electrical contact. Shrouds tend to get clagged up with spatter after a while. Pearls of welding slag may bridge between the tip and shroud, this will lead to very poor performance. Use of a 'spatter release' will lessen the tendency for any slag to stick.

Power Return Lead or 'Earth' and Clamp

Often called the earth lead, this should more properly be known as the power return lead as its job is to return the welding current to the machine. A suitable clamp must be used with the lead; failure to create a good 'earth' will only make welding difficult. Try to prevent the lead from kinking in use, and replace it if it gets hot or if you have any doubts

Gas regulator and valve.

Flux-cored gasless Mig wire.

150 amp gas/no gas machine.

Gasless Mig wire transport system.

Polarity terminals for gas/no gas machine.

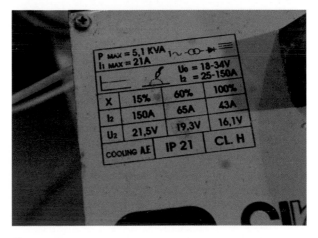

Duty cycle.

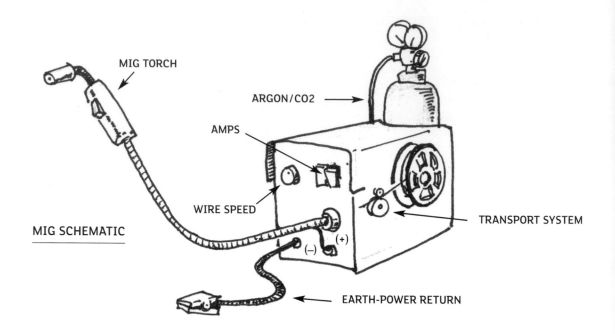

MIG TORCH

ARGON/CO2

AMPS

WIRE SPEED

MIG SCHEMATIC

TRANSPORT SYSTEM

(−)   (+)

EARTH-POWER RETURN

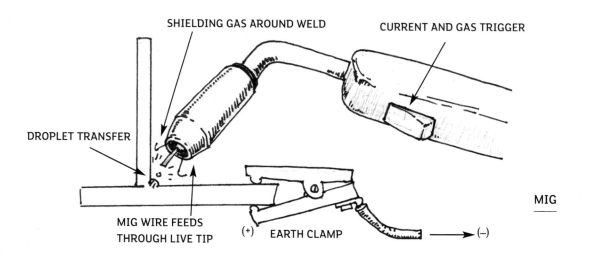

SHIELDING GAS AROUND WELD

CURRENT AND GAS TRIGGER

DROPLET TRANSFER

MIG

MIG WIRE FEEDS
THROUGH LIVE TIP

(+)   EARTH CLAMP   (−)

about its ability to return the power effectively. Keep the clamp clean and ensure the spring is powerful enough to bite through any minor surface rust or dirt.

Gas Bottle and Regulator

Professional welding gas, known as Argoshield, is available from BOC Ltd, who have a national network of depots. Argoshield is a mixture of Argon and CO_2 and comes in a range of ratios which are tailored to specific welding tasks. Argoshield Universal, as the name suggests, is widely used and, unless you are advised otherwise, is probably the one to go for initially.

Gas bottles are rented annually, and the gas is paid for as used. The actual size of bottle is governed by what you are likely to use and by your capacity to handle it. There is no point in renting a huge cumbersome L-cylinder weighing 90kg and standing 1.7m tall if it will take a decade to use up. The Y-cylinder at 93cm and 40kg is far easier to deal with and will do for the semi-professional. The X-cylinder is half the size again. Rental prices are similar, so the main criteria when deciding which bottle to use are its dimensions.

The alternative to rental is to buy disposable or refillable bottles. Several companies supply small bottles of argon or argon CO_2 in disposable bottles. These had a reputation for being unreliable and rather short-lived, but most of the problems have now been ironed out. Anyone wishing to try their hand at Mig welding would do well to consider this an option. Disposable gas bottles retail for about £15. If you intend to take payment for minor welding jobs for friends and family it is probably a good idea to add the cost of a bottle of gas into each job.

Sealey can supply refillable CO_2 bottles on an exchange basis if you first purchase a full bottle. This system is a reasonable compromise between disposable and rental. The initial cost for the bottle is in the region of £60, plus a similar charge for each exchange.

Gasless Mig

The gasless Mig welder is exactly the same as above, but for the absence of the gas bottle and that the polarity of the machine is reversed. In the case of gas/no gas machines, you will have to manually swap the terminals for the torch and return leads, so that the 'earth' is live+ and the torch is 'earthed'−. Flux-cored wire is available only in 0.8mm and comes in 0.7kg reels for about £10 or 5kg for about £45.

CHOOSING A MIG WELDER
Power Rating and Duty Cycle

Mig welders are sold with a power rating in amperes, which should relate to its ability to weld at that stated power output. However, a more realistic guide to any machine's power output is from the duty cycle, which will show what percentage of time the machine is actually running at the stated output for each of the given power settings. The duty cycle is often printed on the machine itself, but will always be published in the blurb which comes with it at point of sale.

Control panel 150 amp welder.

Shown on page 85 is the duty cycle as given on a popular SIP gas/no gas machine, which is rated at 150 amps. A little confusing in its presentation perhaps, the chart shows that at the maximum output of 150 amps the machine is producing that amperage for only 15 per cent of the time and is running at 21.5 volts; while at the lower end of the scale we have 100 per cent power at any setting from 43 amps at 16.1 volts to the lowest of 25 amps.

In real life applications this machine is very good across the board with or without gas.

Big Name vs. No Name

It is understood in some circles that most of the world's Mig welders come from only a handful of factories. As such, you would do well to be guided by a good supplier rather than be swayed by the name on the box. One machine which has been popular and well respected for several decades is the Cebora turbo 130. This very competent little welder has also been sold under the names Murex and Blue Point, and is retailed through BOC and Snap-on respectively at a range of prices. Visit your local BOC gas and gear shop, or go to welduk.com. Motor factors and motorist shops will also carry Mig welders and may turn up a bargain.

Buying Used

It is an odd truth that over the years, many people have purchased Mig welders and then used them only fleetingly. This means that a lot of nearly-new machines are languishing under the stairs of many British households. Assuming the thing has been dry-stored, it will probably work as well as the day it was laid up, needing just a clean and a new reel of wire.

SETTING UP A MIG WELDER

Having purchased a welder, you will need to set it up with gas and wire.

Fitting the Wire

Work with the machine plugged in, but not turned on. A new spool of wire will have the end tucked away somewhere usually through a hole in the drum or under a label. Free this off with care as the wire may try to unwind itself. Trim the end of the wire with side cutters and make sure it does not have a burr which could snag the liner. Straighten the wire for about 10cm – this will make threading it easier.

Place the wire onto the spindle; 5kg spools will require a spacer which should be supplied with the machine. Feed the end of the wire toward the capstan. Most models will have a short length of liner before the capstan, while some will feed directly to it. Undo the quick release on the pinch-wheel, and lift this out of the way. Ensure that the correct groove is in line for the gauge of wire you are using: 0.6 and 0.8 grooves are obviously different and the size will be marked on the outside of the capstan. If need be, swap the capstan by undoing the central Allen bolt or fixing screw. Run the wire over the capstan and feed it into the mouth of the liner for about 15mm.

Replace the pinch-wheel and adjust the tensioner until the wire is secure – too tight and you may experience a snarl-up if the wire burns onto the tip. In such a case you will have to cut the wire and draw it back out of the torch, having first freed it from the tip by 'wiggling'.

Next, remove the shroud and tip from the torch and hold the torch out as straight as possible. Ensure the earth is safely out of the way and that you are not going to place yourself in circuit. Turn on the machine. Press the trigger on the torch and watch as the wire feeds into the liner and up toward the torch. You should now be able to judge if the transport system needs to be adjusted with regard to the pressure on the pinch-wheel.

When the end of the wire emerges from the torch, stop pressing the trigger and fit the tip. The tip is matched to the wire diameter and is fitted with a screw thread; tighten by hand and then nip up with pliers. Trim the wire beyond the tip to about 25mm with side cutters and replace the shroud. Gas shrouds are either threaded or fixed with a helical wire spring.

Connecting the Gas Supply

Full-sized rented bottles will come with a plastic cap or tape over the outlet. Remove this and 'crack' or 'snift' the cylinder – this is done by quickly opening the valve to blow any debris from it. Be certain not to place yourself in the line of fire, and protect your ears.

Attach the regulator by means of the brass gland seal. Many people like to add a line of PTFE tape to the thread, though this is not strictly necessary.

Machines which are rigged for a disposable bottle will need an adapter to run a full-sized bottle – this is available from any welding supply outlet. Disposable bottles are connected via a brass thread to the flow valve, which should be set so as not to release any gas until it is needed.

In use, the shielding gas is run at as low a pressure as is practical to conserve it, and prevents gas bubbles from forming in the weld. Too little gas will lead to a burned joint with poor fusion and a tendency for the wire to melt onto the torch tip. Practice makes perfect.

Good Practice

Get into the habit of turning off the gas immediately after welding and when not in use.

Fabricating a trolley or holder for the gas bottle will make life easier.

Using a spatter-release product – also known as anti-spatter spray – will make cleaning-up around the weld easier by lessening the tendency for any spatter to stick.

Newer water-based formulations will interfere far less with overpainting than the older oil- or silicone-based products.

USING THE MACHINE FOR THE FIRST TIME

Obviously each machine will vary in so far as which power setting/wire speed combination relates to

A BEGINNER'S GUIDE TO MIG WELDING

Everybody will undoubtedly get a jumpy weld the first time they try Mig welding. Having your machine set up properly for the job at hand is 50 per cent of the trick to getting a good weld. A clean tip and nozzle are important, but most of all practice is the key.

Take your time to get used to the sparking and the way the arc starts. With your welding visor on, don't be afraid to look at the arc. In order to produce a good weld you need to see what the wire's doing at the weld pool, so that you can 'stir' it effectively – this is moving the wire within the weld pool to get it to flow where you want it to. For the most part this just means moving the torch from one piece to the other across the joint.

But let's start at the beginning. Cut some test pieces and clamp them in place to form an overlapping joint. With a new or clean tip and nozzle, turn your gas on. You generally want it set at around 5psi, though if you're working in a breeze you might need to turn it up onc.

Secure your earth clamp to a good clean area of the piece you're welding to, and turn the machine on. For most things you probably want to start on the 1-max (2nd of 4) setting with the wire speed up around 7 or 8 (of 10), but if you're welding thicker metal you'll need to turn power and speed up, or down for thinner metal. With practice you'll know where your machine needs to be set to get the desired results.

So with the gas set to 5psi, the power to 1-max (2nd position of 4) and the wire speed to about 7.5 (out of 10) put your visor on, point the tip at the joint you want to weld and hold it approximately 2–2.5mm away from the piece. Pull the trigger and watch the weld; with a few tries to get used to it all you should be able to draw a line of weld that doesn't jump or bounce.

Next practise the speed at which you draw the line – if you go too slow it'll drop out and melt a hole in your piece; too fast and it'll be dotty. Try to make the weld pool flow evenly along the seam.

What we tend to do to get a nice even join is to pulse weld: this is a series of overlapping lines of weld, basically doing a bit at a time instead of trying to get across the seam in one go. By pulsing the weld you give the metal just a little extra time to cool so you're less likely to have your molten weld pool drop out. Practise this till you think you've got the hang of it, then practise some more. When you've mastered that, move on to a right angle joint and practise some more.

Then eventually move on to practise a butt joint. Butt joints are more prone to burning holes, but don't worry if you do burn through your piece, just turn the power down and weld around the hole you've burned to create a reinforced edge, then bridge across the hole by working your way around the inside edge of the reinforcing with more weld. With practice, when it's ground back it'll be unnoticeable

THINGS TO LOOK OUT FOR

Weld jumps and wire burns back:	power and speed are too high
Weld jumps but wire flows normally:	wire speed is too high
Weld blows hole straight through piece:	power too high
Wire melts back to tip:	wire is too slow
Weld is 'gassy', bubbly and blobby:	gas is set too high
Weld is glazed, burnt and very brittle:	gas is set too low

which gauge of metal, but as a rule you should select the lowest power setting and a middling wire speed to try the thing out on a clean piece of 18 or 20swg. First balance the wire to get an even deposition of metal and then move the power up one notch at a time until the optimum weld is found.

Listen for a clean 'ripping' sound, which is rather like a cross between thunder and the tearing of fresh linen. Failure for the weld to initiate cleanly may be due to the following: too low an amperage, poor earth, or from holding the torch too far from the work or at too shallow an angle. You may also find your hand being pushed back by the wire as it issues from the tip.

5kg reel has wire fed into liner and onto…

…groove in capstan.

Access to capstan if groove incorrect.

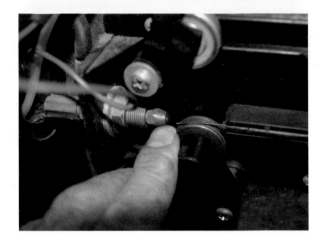

Wire fed across capstan…

INSTALLING WELDING WIRE

In welding there are several variables which have to be balanced. These are: (1) wire speed, (2) current, (3) length of wire beyond tip, (4) speed of movement across workpiece and (5) quality of 'earth' power return.

CREATING MIG WELDS

Mig Stud Weld

Commonly and mistakenly referred to as a Mig spot, the stud weld is used to fix panels in place of the original resistance spot welds which are a feature of vehicle manufacture. The weld is formed by drilling or punching a hole through on a piece of metal which is then laid onto another. The Mig is fed through the hole and fuses with the lower sheet before flowing into and fusing with the top. Aim the wire at the centre of the hole and pull the trigger for a second or so; then at the last moment by giving the torch a little 'stir', you can encourage better fusion with both pieces.

Mig Spot Weld

The true Mig spot weld is not seen very often, as it is unpredictable in its results. The join is formed by laying two sheets together and then aiming the torch squarely at the top one. The idea is to weld through both sheets to form a 'spot' of weld.

…and into liner of torch.

With tensioner replace the wire.

Wire feeds through torch and tip is replaced.

Shroud replaced and wire trimmed.

Drilling a hole in the top sheet as above is just as easy, and allows you to see the weld forming.

Stitch Weld

Set up a couple of pieces of 20swg to join. Aim at the middle of the seam and trigger for a couple of seconds while moving at an even speed across the metal from right to left. Take care not to move the torch away from the job under the influence of the wire, which will tend to push. Hold the torch at approx 45 degrees to the seam in both planes. You will find angles to suit your own hand – too shallow an angle will mean that the wire will tend to bounce off while initiating a weld; too sharp

Welder is ready to work.

A BEGINNER'S GUIDE TO GASLESS MIG

Using a gasless Mig welder is pretty much as above, but with the polarity on the torch and earth clamp swapped around so that you have a positive earth and negative torch, and obviously you don't have to worry about turning on the gas or setting the regulator.

With a gasless machine you put in your gasless wire, swap the torch and earth leads around – this is usually a pair of external terminals on the front of the machine that simply undo and swap over, though on some machines they may be under the side cover, accessible when you change your wire spool. Gasless or flux-cored wire is not available in 0.6mm, so if that is your standard (which it should be) you will have to fit the 0.8 sides of the capstan and a 0.8 tip to your torch.

The flux in the gasless wire produces a white smoky deposit and a light brown coloured crust over the weld that can be easily removed with a wire brush afterwards. Because of the amount of smoke and spatter produced by the flux it's not as easy to see what the weld pool is doing, when compared with a standard Mig.

Welding over the same spot after the pool has cooled does not work well without prior cleaning. The flux does not conduct well, making pulse welding less suitable; instead using a zigzag stirring pattern and aiming to get right across the seam in one go is the best way to get good results using gasless wire. For this reason a lot of practice on test pieces is advisable.

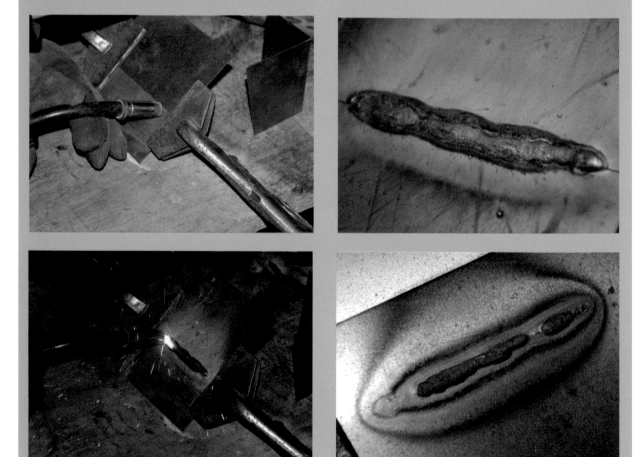

Butt weld using gasless Mig. Bottom right: Heat penetration behind weld.

*Outdoor welding.
Left: Typical kit.
Below: Area clear,
safe to start.*

*Above: Work begins to
repair hinge.*

*Right: Catch is built
up with weld.*

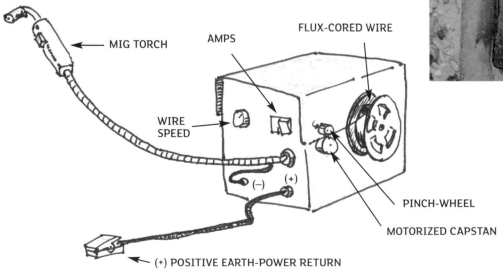

GASLESS MIG SCHEMATIC

MIG TORCH

AMPS

FLUX-CORED WIRE

WIRE
SPEED

(−)   (+)

PINCH-WHEEL

MOTORIZED CAPSTAN

(+) POSITIVE EARTH-POWER RETURN

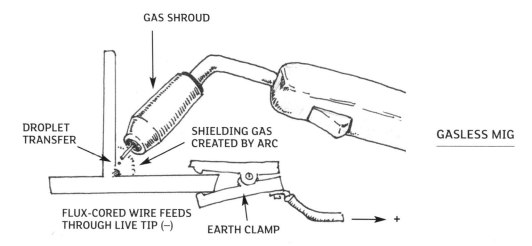

GAS SHROUD

DROPLET
TRANSFER

SHIELDING GAS
CREATED BY ARC

GASLESS MIG

FLUX-CORED WIRE FEEDS
THROUGH LIVE TIP (–)   EARTH CLAMP   +

an angle may tend to stab the wire through the weld pool.

Check for even and thorough penetration on the other side of the test piece. Once you are competent with this, practise working from left to right with the torch held in the same position. In time you will be able to trigger the torch using your thumb whilst working overhead.

String of Pearls Welding

A run of overlapping tacks is known as a 'string of pearls'. This is a method of forming a joint which reduces heat build-up and so lessens distortion – and the risk of burning through the workpiece. This trick is ideal for laying in vehicle floor panels and a million other applications.

RISKS/SAFETY CONSIDERATIONS

- The Mig is a heavy and cumbersome machine with a pressurized gas bottle attached to it. The process is powered by the mains and involves the generation of an electric arc. During the welding process, sparks and globules of molten metal issue from the torch, along with a gas which is an oxygen depletor.
- There is an obvious fire risk and a less obvious problem with stray sparks which can lead to smouldering and the chance of a flare-up many hours after working has ceased.
- All fumes produced by the process should be treated as toxic, especially when welding galvanized steel, as there is a risk of metal fume

fever from the zinc. Gasless flux-cored wire will produce gaseous ozone which is known to cause delayed damage to lungs. An extractor is advised, as is a suitable breathing mask.
- The arc will produce radiation burns as well as damaging visible light.
- Residual heat in welded metal is a constant hazard, as the temptation to pick up and admire your work is often too strong.
- When using any electrical device with an extension lead, be sure to fully uncoil the cable so as to reduce impedance and the risk of overheating.

State of the art dual-purpose Mig has aluminium and braze set-ups.

Beautiful Tig welding.

CHAPTER 10

Tig Welding

Tig (tungsten inert gas) welding is a form of electrical arc welding, in which an earthed tungsten electrode is held in close proximity to the live workpiece and an arc is generated between them. The very localized heat allows pure fusion of two pieces of metal, with or without additional filler material. A shielding gas is used to displace oxygen from the immediate weld area. Unlike other forms of arc welding, the tungsten electrode is not consumed in the process.

There are two sorts of Tig welders, AC and DC. The new generation of 'DC inverter' Tig machines has brought the cost of Tig into the reach of the home restorer and into competition with the previously ubiquitous Mig. Tig welding can produce welds of the highest quality, but is far more demanding in terms of skill and time. (AC Tig welders are capable of welding light alloys and aluminium, but they are far more costly and so not really suitable for the enthusiast or hobbyist.)

WHAT METALS CAN IT JOIN?

In theory, Tig is capable of welding any metal – but for our purposes DC Tig is primarily for joining mild or stainless steel.

WHAT IS IT USED FOR?

Tig is a pure fusion technique, unlike the Mig, which relies on metal transfer from the electrode. Tig welding is by its nature slower than both Mig and gas welding, but has advantages over each. Firstly, as a pure fusion method there is less excess material left at the site of the weld, and this allows for hammer welding. The process involves a softer, more gentle arc and produces less spatter than Mig,

and when compared with gas, does not have the invisible flame and gives less heat soak and therefore less heat distortion.

In practice, it is unlikely that Tig on its own will satisfy all of your welding requirements and so is best used in conjunction with Mig.

ALSO KNOWN AS?

(Just to confuse, some of the names are common to the Mig welder.)
- Tig (tungsten inert gas) refers to the tungsten electrode and the inert shielding gas argon. Argon welding and argon arc welding are both terms that have been applied to Mig welding.
- TAGS (tungsten arc gas shielded) is accurate if not elegant, while GSTA (gas shielded tungsten arc) trips off the tongue.

HOW DOES IT WORK?

Tig welders will be derived from MMA (stick) welders – an MMA machine with an added torch and connections for a gas bottle. The DC Tig welder is essentially a transformer (inverter) and a gas bottle. Attached to this are a torch (earth–) and an earth lead (pos+). The gas bottle will have a regulator and ideally a flow meter. Control for the current may be on the machine, the torch, or a separate foot pedal. Better machines will feature controls for slope-in, which is the rate at which the current picks up when activated, and HF (high frequency) start.

If the tungsten electrode on the torch is touched to the earthed workpiece, and the current applied, a circuit will exist. If we then scratch the metal surface and lift the electrode slightly off the workpiece, an arc should be generated as the current continues

Typical inverter control panel.

Tig/MMA function switch.

ANATOMY OF THE TIG WELDER

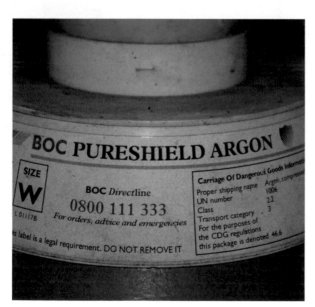

Above: Pureshield argon in full sized bottle.

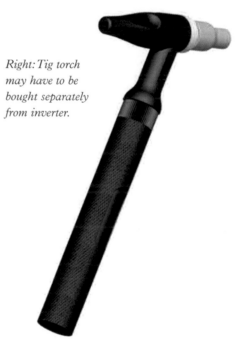

Right: Tig torch may have to be bought separately from inverter.

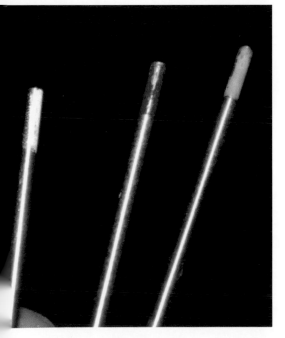

Above left: Gas regulator and flow meter.

Above right: Disposable gas bottles for low-consumption users.

Left: Red thoriated, white zirconated and grey ceriated tungsten electrodes.

Above: Tig torch in bits: handle and gas shroud, with tungsten electrode and collet.

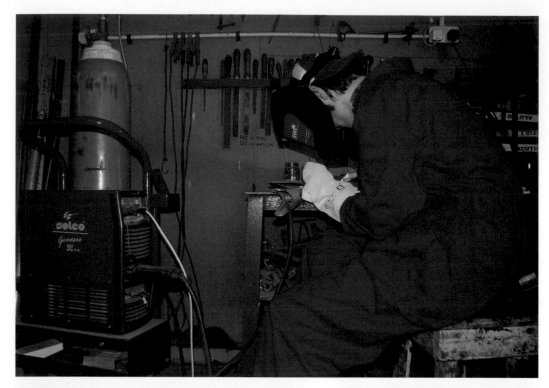

Typical workstation.

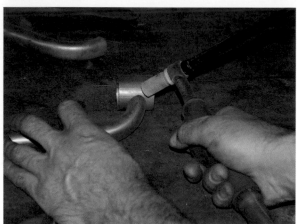

Power grip in use.

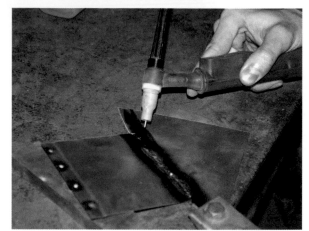

Looser grip.

to flow across the air gap. This process is known as a scratch start – it works, but can be refined. Machines which are designed to be primarily MMA welders will tend to produce a high power pulse in response to the electrode contacting the workpiece; this can have the effect of overheating a small area of the metal. One method of avoiding this is to place a small scrap of sheet on the work-piece and to initiate the arc on it – when the arc is stable you can move it off and begin welding in earnest.

HF start gives a more subtle beginning to the arc as it switches the current many times a second. The foot control allows the power to be controlled as the heat builds in the weld area. The high frequency must only be used to initiate the arc, as it may

First-hand lessons are invaluable.

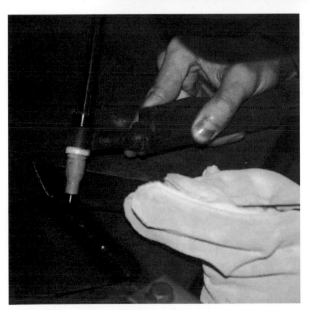

Filler rod ready to be fed into weld.

induce a current and 'tracking' which can damage electrical coils in other equipment. HF is also known to interfere with communication and radio equipment.

Lift start (also known as 'lift Tig') is a new development in which, as the name suggests, the electrode is touched to the workpiece and simply lifted off to initiate the arc. Lift Tig relies on a feedback loop and is now to be found on the better low-priced machines.

The pure argon shielding gas is used to displace oxygen from the weld area and to cool it.

Power Source

The power source for Tig welding is a compact box which may come with a shoulder strap. Older and more powerful machines will be wheel mounted and are generally a lot larger. The unit will have all the relevant controls, which will vary depending on the sophistication of the particular model.

A BEGINNER'S GUIDE TO THE TIG WELDER

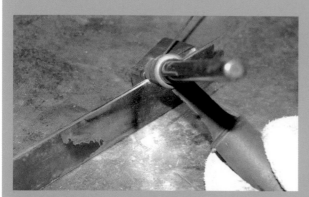

Set to weld.

Contact.

Tig is less tolerant of impurities in and around the site of weld and so demands that the area be thoroughly cleaned, and that you wear cotton or latex gloves. Make sure your electrode tip is clean, and clean up the edges of your seam with a wire brush or emery paper. Before starting and after each weld, remove any oxidization or carbon deposits.

With a 'thoriated' tungsten tip (filed to a 20–30 degree point) in the torch and the gas turned on, secure your earth clamp to your piece and switch on your welder. If you're using a foot pedal control then the power controls on your machine will be set to the maximum power your foot pedal will go up to, so set them slightly higher than you want, to give you room to balance the power, holding the pedal where you want it rather than just pressing it all the way down like a switch.

Put your visor on and hold the torch around 3mm away from the seam at a similar angle to how you would hold a pencil (around 30 degrees from flat). Now slowly depress the foot pedal – the gas will start to flow and it will hum, but nothing will happen to begin with. Keep going until an arc is established – a blue bolt of lightning will jump from the torch onto the piece. Hold the torch steady and increase the power on the foot pedal slightly – the arc should start to heat the metal where it strikes.

Practise starting the arc like this till you've got the hang of it – too quickly and your torch will cut out; too slowly and the arc will have trouble establishing. Be careful not to make contact with the tip on the piece,

and take notice of the condition of the tip, as the more it is used the more it will burn or melt away.

Now try to aim the arc so that it strikes just on the edge of one side of your seam. Move it very slightly, so that it now hits the other side of the seam. Move the tip so that your arc hits on one side, then the other in a fine zigzag pattern. With practice the edges will melt and fuse together. Work your way along the seam melting and flowing the edges together, reducing the power slightly as you go, so as to account for the heat building up in the piece. Feed in filler rod with your other hand where necessary to bridge holes.

Tig welding has a 'soft' arc and is one of the more controlled methods of welding. With practice the results can be beautiful. If you're familiar with gas welding and Mig welding then you will likely relate easily to the Tig process, as Tig is essentially a cross between the two.

Scratch start: Using a scratch start Tig is a similar but slightly less controlled process. In order to establish an arc you must actually make contact with the tip of your torch and draw it across the metal, then lift the torch away to create an arc. You'll need to practise this so as not to damage your pieces as the arc is established. One trick is to attach a scrap of metal to your piece for establishing the arc on (you later discard the scrap).

Lift Tig or lift start: Machines which feature the new lift Tig start will prove to be the easiest for the novice welder, as this system does not give rise to a hot-spot where the tungsten touches.

Once the arc is started your power is constant – so you can't adjust it, to compensate for heat soak. With this in mind, try not to take too long to get across the

Controlling arc as weld progresses.

Gap is filled with rod.

Weld is complete – note effects of heat.

seam or your weld pool may drop out. Spend less time moving the torch between the seams as you go, as your pool will establish quicker as things progress. If you need to, stop. Wait for the piece to cool down, clean up your edges and then continue.

A basic inverter which might be primarily designed as an MMA welder, but with the facility for a Tig conversion, as seen here, will have controls for MMA/Tig, output power, mains switch, and two 'dinse' plug sockets to accept the welding and return leads. The dinse plugs in use are essentially bayonet-type fixings which come in one of two sizes for this type of machine, depending on power range.

Optional Controls and Settings

More expensive machines will offer the use of a foot pedal switch which allows the current to be fine-tuned during the welding process. In practice, the foot control is only really of use when working at a bench. It is used to back off the current if the weld pool is in danger of overheating, or to 'feather' the current at the end of a run, which lessens the chance of leaving a hollow – as this can lead to cracking.

The other setting which will be found on better machines is the 'slope-in/slope-out'. This provides for a smooth rise in current at the start of welding and a gradual drop-off at the end. Slope-in/out is a more useable alternative to the foot pedal as it can be employed in any situation.

The Torch and Leads

The welding lead will house the power cable and gas pipe. MMA-based machines will usually have the gas bottle adapter as part of the lead. This will most likely be sized to accept a disposable bottle, and will need a further adapter if a full-sized cylinder is to be employed. Better leads will feature a gas tap near to the torch, along with a switch for the welding current.

The torch itself is made up of the electrode, holder, ceramic gas shroud and a handle. The grip employed in Tig welding is not as intuitive as with Mig, and so will need some practice before the power is actually switched on. You may opt for the power-grip or use a pen-grip for more delicate work.

In order to keep a constant arc, the electrode must be held at an even 2.5mm distance from the workpiece. Accidental touching of the electrode tip will demand that it be reground to the correct profile. The electrode is held in a brass collet which allows for removal and repositioning.

TIG ELECTRODE SIZES

Diameter will increase with current. This is a rough guide. Consult your supplier and the specification of your particular machine.

Current	Diameter
5–35 amps	1.6mm
30–100 amps	2mm
100–160 amps	2.4mm

ELECTRODE TIP ANGLES

Current	Angle
5–30 amps	30 degrees
30–90 amps	30–120 degrees
90–120 amps	120–160 degrees

Again, this is a rough guide and you would do well to consult your supplier or the spec sheet from your particular machine.

Tungsten electrodes come in three basic varieties and are colour coded:

Red tip Thoriated tungsten is used for welding mild and stainless steel.
White tip Zirconated tungsten used for welding aluminium.
Grey tip Ceriated tungsten is used to weld both steel and aluminium, and works particularly well with inverter machines.

Welding Filler Rod

A full range of filler rods is available providing grades of steel and other metals closely matched to the material being joined. For our purpose, a general grade of steel will usually suffice. Some grades of 'duplex' stainless steel will allow for dissimilar grades to be welded. Rod is supplied in 1.6 mm, 2.4mm and 3.3mm diameter. An alternative is to cut thin slices from the sheet which you are working with, and use these to fill with. Brazing and bronze welding rods are also available which can be pre-fluxed.

Tig rods must be stored in clean, dry and weatherproof conditions.

Grinder

A bench grinder has to be considered as an integral part of the Tig welding set-up, especially when starting out. The profile or point of the tungsten electrode will vary depending on the current used. If too sharp a profile is selected, then the tip will overheat and melt. Too soft, and it will not produce an arc of the correct intensity. The profile is also varied depending on the exact make-up of the electrode.

Power Return Lead

The power return lead or earth is live during the Tig process and as such must be connected to the pos+ terminal dinse socket. The earth clamp must be clean and securely bitten onto the workpiece or bench in a manner which provides a good electrical connection to the point of weld.

CHOOSING A TIG WELDER

The new generation of inverter machines has brought Tig into the reach of the small workshop and home restorer. The least expensive will be sold primarily as MMA welders with an optional Tig lead, which will include a gas coupling. A regulator/flow meter and adapter will usually have to be purchased separately for connection to a full-size bottle.

Look at machines rated at 100–200 amps, with 140/150 as the probable optimum. Industrial welding suppliers will carry a range of Tig inverters which are undoubtedly brilliant but not aimed at the non-professional. Contact your local independent welding supply shop or go to www.welduk.com. Inverters begin at about £200 plus the cost of a torch and gas. Expect to pay in the region of £300 upwards to start Tig welding.

SHIELDING GAS

Pure argon is the usual shielding gas used in Tig welding. It is available for sale in disposable bottles or in large industrial cylinders, which are rented from BOC and the gas paid for as used. Your choice of cylinder should be based upon your expected consumption. 'Pureshield' argon is available in a range of bottle sizes which all cost about the same –

What should you pay?

the largest, W at 146cm tall and 85kg, are rather unwieldy and more trouble than they are worth unless you expect to get through an awful lot of gas. More realistic options are the 93cm tall X and Y sizes at 19 and 40 kg respectively.

AC TIG

AC Tig machines are considerably more expensive than DC units and are only advantageous if you wish to work with aluminium or some of the more exotic light alloys. As the name suggests the AC welder produces an arc in which the current switches polarity many times in a second. AC units are capable of DC output and will usually offer the option of use with a foot pedal. AC machines currently retail from about £1200.

Tig consumables.

AC Tig welder control panel. More complex than simple inverter machine.

SETTING UP THE TIG WELDER

The SIP inverter shown here is typical of the entry level Tig set-up, sold as an MMA machine with an optional Tig torch and disposable argon bottle. The front panel has dinse sockets for the power leads, which must be correctly connected for the chosen method of use.

The disposable argon bottle is simply screwed into the adapter and is controlled from the torch. A full-sized bottle requires a further adapter and a regulator/flow meter (available from BOC, Sealey, Weld UK, or from your local welding supplies outlet); unlike Mig, the Tig flow meter shows the rate of gas flow and not simply the pressure.

The torch is supplied ready to go, though it pays to become familiar with its set-up as you will no doubt be taking the electrode out very soon in order to regrind its profile.

Your new welder will probably come with a chipping hammer and a rudimentary face mask. Another vital piece of equipment is a wire brush.

RISKS/SAFETY CONSIDERATIONS

- The Tig welder is a heavy and cumbersome machine with a pressurized gas bottle attached to it. Inverter Tig machines are smaller and easier to handle than their older counterparts.
- Fumes from Tig welding are considered as toxic, especially when dealing with galvanized or coated steel which may produce metal fume fever. Tig generates gaseous ozone which is known to cause delayed lung damage. The pure

Aluminium Tig welding.

argon shielding gas is not toxic, but is an oxygen depletor and as such is an asphyxiant. Argon is colourless, odourless and is heavier than air. BOC will provide you with the necessary gas handling and safety information.

● This device is mains operated and produces an electrical arc. The arc produces visible light which can cause permanent damage to sight and also radiation which will cause burns to skin. The process also creates white-hot sparks. It is possible for the operator to place himself in circuit with the welder and receive an electrical shock.

● All welding processes involve heating metal parts which take time to cool.

● Tig welders which employ a high frequency start are known to interfere with some electronic devices and to cause damage to electrical windings.

● Any person with a pacemaker or related medical condition should take advice from their doctor before engaging in the use of this type of machinery.

Mechanical fixings.

CHAPTER 11

Alternatives to Welding

While we are primarily concerned with welding, brazing and soldering, it is important to understand and consider the alternatives, such as mechanical fixings and adhesives.

MECHANICAL FIXINGS

Welding, wherein one piece is fused with another to create a new whole, might be considered the ultimate form of mechanical fixing. But fixings of all sorts, both temporary and permanent, are all around us. Buttons, Velcro and magnets can be thought of as mechanical attachment methods, though nuts, bolts and spire clips are more usually employed for metalwork applications. It pays to be aware of the range available as this will provide options and flexibility with the design and construction of any projects.

Rivets, for example, are wrongly considered by many to be a redundant method of fabrication. A look around should show you otherwise. Cold rivets have been used to build and repair aircraft since the dawn of flight, and are still commonly used. On a slightly larger scale hot rivets were the chosen method of fabricating ships' hulls from the industrial revolution to the Second World War. Victorian engineers employed rivets of all types to change the world. Modern pop rivets are widely used as temporary fixings in car restoration and repair, and also in the fabrication of modern lightweight vehicles.

Likewise nuts and bolts go back to the beginnings of engineering, but should never be ruled out as current technique. Nutsert fixings combine the best qualities of screw fixings with those of the pop rivet. Investing in the correct tool could save many hours of welding. If you are not familiar with the system, you would probable never consider it. Spire clips and the like allow screw threads to be used to join sheetwork without any specialist tools.

The range of fixings is large and ever growing, so

Assorted PK screws.

Panhead screw. Broad flat head dissipates the load better than standard screw.

Nutsert fixing.

it's a good idea to check out your local fixing centre or the catalogues at your motor factors. Here are a few of the types of fixings you might use as an alternative or complement to your welding.

Nuts and Bolts

Nuts and bolts are the very beginning of engineering; your local motor factor or DIY store will sell a good range of sizes that will do for most applications. Specialist fixing shops carry a mind-boggling array of goods, including obscure threads and high tensile items for specialist and historic machinery. Tap and die sets allow you to renovate and replace missing parts and to fabricate your own captives.

Captive Nuts and Spire Clips

When fixing a nut to a washer or inside a panel, it is standard practice to place an appropriate bolt into the nut whilst welding. This ensures that the thread does not distort or clag up with spatter, and can often help with location. Do not weld a captive

washer all the way around as this may actually weaken the panel rather than increase its strength.

Nutsert Fixings

This clever system fixes a 'nut' into any panel. Quick, easy, and without damage to the surrounding metalwork or paint, the Nutsert has a million uses and is as easy to install as a pop rivet. Nutserts are available in a range of sizes from tool and fixing suppliers.

PK Self-Tapping Screws

Used widely as temporary fixings in bodywork, the self-tapper should be a staple in any workshop. A selection box can be acquired from any motorist shop or DIY centre. Pan-head screws spread the load well and so are favoured for panel fixing.

Dzus Fasteners

The Dzus quarter-turn screw can be found on historic aircraft and modern hotrods. Highly practical, they give any job an air of class.

Pop Rivets

Pop rivets are available in a huge variety of types and sizes. 1/8th pops are the standard temporary fixing for setting up panels in crash repair of motor vehicles. The same fixings are widely used to fabricate Box vans. Bifurcated rivets are designed to split and will apply little or no pressure to the side of the hole, while lost head or countersunk rivets sit flush. Pop rivets come in aluminium, stainless or mild steel; consult your stockist for the full range.

Cold Rivets

Still employed in aeroplane construction, the cold rivet is used in conjunction with a 'bucking bar' and an air-powered hammer. This process usually involves two operators – one to hold the bucking bar inside the structure and one to bring the hammer to bear. The hammer will have a hollow in its head that will form the domed mushroom shape that will hold the two panels together. Cold rivets can be beaten over by hand with a hammer. Fine for suits of armour, but this method would not be deemed suitable for high tolerance work such as above.

SPREADING THE LOAD

When creating any sort of joint you must consider the stresses involved and where they will act. Penny washers and spreader plates are often used to dissipate a load.

Nutsert tool.

Insert on tool.

Insert in hole.

Insert 'pulled'.

NUTSERT FIXING

This clever device is a captive thread with a million uses.

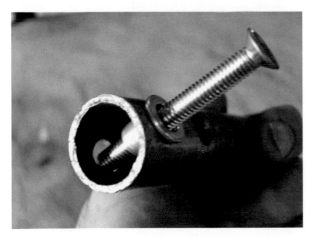

Screw in insert.

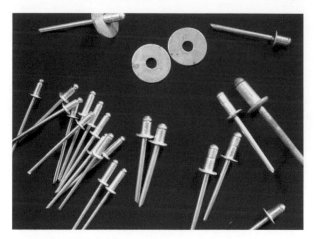

A selection of rivets and washers.

Choose rivet by diameter, depth and head size/shape.

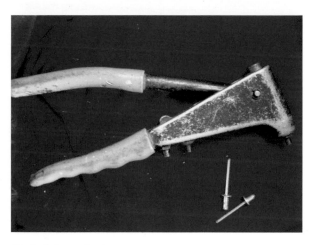

Typical domestic rivet gun.

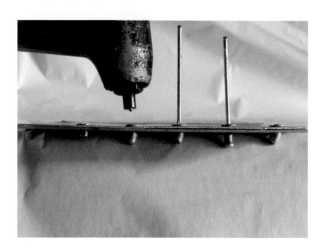

Stages of pulling a pop rivet.

POP RIVETS

Clamps, Mole-Grips etc.

While fabricating welded structures the use of clamps is essential; you can never have too many clamps and the more options the better. Weights, magnets, sandbags and old jacks will often save the day. Some new high-quality items will be required – the new self-adjusting type clamps are brilliant, but there will be times when a clamp will be sacrificed during work, so a few 'not so good' clamps are also a good idea. Auto jumbles are a good source of old tools at low prices.

ADHESIVES

Joining metals with adhesive is not a new concept. At least as far back as the eighteenth century, it was normal to bond the iron/steel tang of a sword blade to a wooden handle with hot pitch. In the same way, polyurethane bonding sealer will stick pretty much anything to anything and will even draw residual moisture out of a joint as it goes off. This property makes it ideal for gluing and sealing metal bits in applications where rigidity is not an issue.

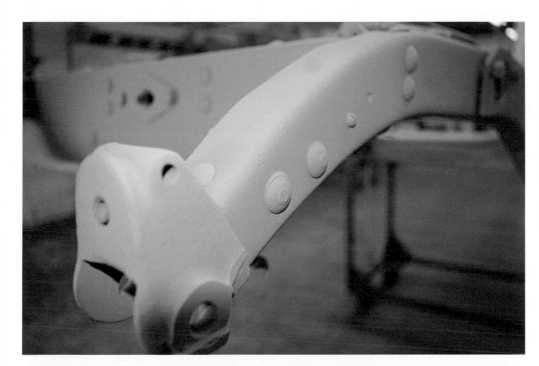

Left: Riveted construction: hot rivets contract as they cool to add rigidity to a structure.

Below: 1930s vehicle chassis.

Superglues have become common in a wide range of applications from surgery to jewellery-making, and are well known for their ability to join many metals. Likewise, epoxy resins are often used when restoring priceless metal artefacts such as statuary, because the join is not necessarily permanent. Should a more suitable technology emerge the resin can be dissolved leaving the option to effect a better repair.

The use of metal-to-metal glues has become commonplace over the last thirty years or so. During this time we have been promised many compounds that claim to rival welding in their ability to bond metals. While many products do work very successfully on small-scale jobs, it is unlikely that anyone is going to glue together an aluminium ladder or steel bookshelf.

Many motor manufacturers now employ combination rivet/bonding-sealer joins to mount panels onto structural members – this method utilizes the high tensile strength of the flexible polyurethane sealer with the rigid fixing ability of the rivet. Dissimilar metals, and those which do not lend themselves easily to welding, can be used in this way to reduce overall weight considerably.

Metals in general have smooth non-porous surfaces which do not easily lend themselves to being 'glued'. As a result we tend to opt for an adhesive which gives a degree of chemical bonding. Cyanoacrylate superglues and polyurethane bonding sealer both rely on water molecules to form a bond, and indeed, the latter is useful in vehicle work for drawing moisture out of joins as it cures. As a rule though, you want to remove any water from a joint to be glued. 'Keying' a smooth surface has the effect of adding some grip and increasing the surface area on a microscopic scale. Abrading a metal surface should also remove oxides, which might impede the bonding process.

Superglues

Superglues are useful for fiddly jobs such as jewellery work, but their low shear-strength limits the scale of join. Q-bond is a proprietary bonding system, which comes with a dry powder that is used as a filler. This is good for countless jobs that require gaps to be filled or parts to be built up. Applying pressure during the bonding process is essential to gain the maximum strength from any superglue.

Hot Glue Gun

Hot glue guns are handy, as they allow the gluing of pretty much anything to anything. Useful for low-strength applications, the hot glue will not usually give rise to any distortion or discoloration of painted surfaces.

Epoxy Resin

Epoxy resin two-part adhesives are relatively high strength glues that rely on more material in any given joint than superglues, and therefore usually have more body. Also sold as many of the 'wonder-weld' products that claim to mimic the qualities of cast-iron, epoxy cannot really be regarded as a substitute for metal.

Panel Kits

Several manufacturers have produced panel adhesive kits that are designed to replace welding – these allow for panel sections to be set in place with an overlap. Careful use of clamps and temporary fixing is required – as once the glue has set, it is rigid.

Polyurethane Bonding Sealer

Polyurethane (PU) bonding sealer is widely used as adhesive and seam sealer in the motor manufacture and repair industries. This material is applied from a sealer gun and will take several hours to cure fully, during which time it may need support. PU sealer actively draws moisture out of a joint, which makes it ideal for restoration projects and cases where water ingress would lead to deterioration. Polyurethane does not provide rigid fixing and so its use must be considered carefully because, as a rule, when this stuff is stuck, it's really stuck.

RISKS / SAFETY CONSIDERATIONS

- All of the above adhesives will glue skin, clothing and eyelids.
- Most are toxic, and all can give rise to fumes.
- Pay close attention to the manufacturer's guidelines, and take care not to transfer any material to where it is not wanted.

Adhesives have been used for hundreds of years to bond metal.

Old sword blade is held with pitch between tang and handle.

Cyanoacrylate superglue is now familiar.

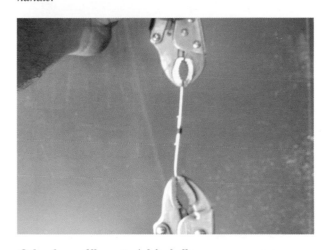

Q-bond uses filler material for bulk.

Hot-glue gun.

Low strength applications can be fixed with chemical adhesives.

A typical soldered joint for domestic plumbing.

CHAPTER 12

Soft Soldering for Domestic Plumbing

Soft soldering is used in domestic plumbing to join copper pipes. Copper is a very good conductor of heat and has a high heat (absorption) capacity. These qualities demand that the heat source used in forming a soldered joint be far greater than a domestic iron. Propane or mapp gas torches are ideal, though an oxy-acetylene set could also be employed with care.

The fiercer heat source in turn creates the need for more active (acidic) fluxes to be used in order to control the formation of oxides on the copper surface. These more active and therefore more toxic fluxes must be removed for reasons of safety if the pipes provide 'potable' water. For the same reason, only lead-free solders should be used.

When joining copper pipe to either copper or brass fittings, it is essential that the solder flows thoroughly to ensure a strong and watertight joint. Obviously, some pipes might carry gas or oil, and failure to seal a joint could prove catastrophic in these cases.

ALSO KNOWN AS?

- Pipe fitting or simply fitting.
- The type of joint is commonly known as sweat-soldering. Sweating refers to the capillary action which draws the solder into the close-fitting joint. Un-sweating is the reverse process by which we can undo a joint if need be.

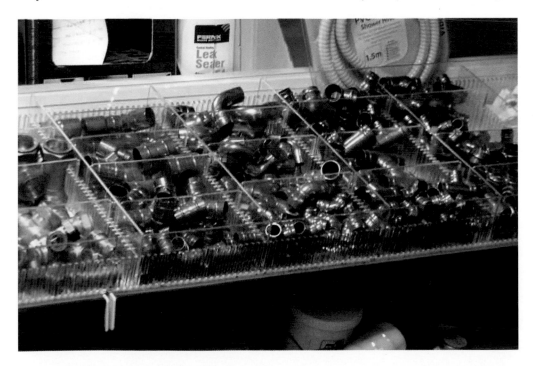

Wide range of fittings sold by high street outlet.

Typical soldered joints used in domestic plumbing.

IN A NUTSHELL

Copper Piping

Traditionally copper pipes came in two types: rigid and soft. The softer variety is essentially rigid pipe which has been annealed to counter the work-hardening effect of 'drawing', which is part of the manufacturing process. As such, soft pipe is the more expensive. Recently a 'half-hard' grade of pipe has come to be seen as the standard. Half-hard pipe will not bend to the same degree as soft, but will cope with some tweaking.

Fittings

The process uses one of two types of fitting: (1) an end-feed or standard fitting, which needs to be 'fed' with solder to create a join; or (2) a 'Yorkshire solder ring', which has a bulge containing pre-loaded solder. Both demand that the pipe be cleaned thoroughly before it is inserted into the sleeve of the joint, and both require that the pipe and joint be evenly heated to a temperature where the solder will flow.

Heat

Propane or mapp gas (LPG) torches are ideal, though an oxy-acetylene set could also be employed with care. The best blowtorches for this type of work are self-igniting, as they give you a free hand and allow you to put the thing down safely.

End-feed or standard type corner fitting.

Yorkshire solder ring type corner fitting.

Propane is cheaper than mapp gas, but does not produce as hot a flame. The economics are slewed slightly by a hotter flame, meaning that the job is done more quickly with less gas used.

Solder

While the leaded variety tends to be easier to work with as it flows better, this is not to be used on potable water. Your supplier will carry a few grades of solder in lead or lead-free formulations. As an alternative a wide range of solder-free compression joints is also available from DIY stores and plumbers' merchants.

Flux

A range of fluxes are available, some of which claim to be self-cleaning – which is to say there is no need to remove the oxide layer from the pipe prior to soldering. Professional plumbers will routinely use wire wool for this job, regardless which flux is used.

The flux is applied with a brush to the end of the pipe inside and out, and to the inside of the fitting.

So called 'solder flux pastes' contain an amount of solder and claim to improve the bond. These work rather like a solder-paint in that they pre-tin the joint before the solder is applied. Ask at your local suppliers for the best solder/flux combination for your exact requirement. Removal of excess flux after joining is advisable to avoid subsequent corrosion to pipes and fittings.

Heat Shield

As many of the joints will need to be soldered in close proximity to walls, doors and ceilings, a heat shield of some sort is required. The plumber's mat is relatively cheap and will do for most applications. Aluminium sheet or a metallic heat sink may also be employed.

Joints

A wide range of solder-free compression joints is also available from DIY stores and plumbers' merchants.

A welding exercise to demonstrate heat distortion.

CHAPTER 13

Controlling Heat Distortion

It is a well-known phenomenon that metal objects will expand when heated and return to normal size as they cool down again. What is less well known is that if you were to heat (for example) a piece of steel tube until a small area glowed red, the tube would expand as you might expect; but if you then allowed it to cool naturally, the area which had previously been red would contract beyond its original size. Now if that red area had been to one side of the tube only, then the tube would quite likely take on a slight bend centred at the previously hottest point.

This quality can be put to good use in some situations, but in others it is at very least a nuisance. Both thermal expansion and contraction must be accounted for when joining metal with heat, if we are to obtain predictable results. Bracing with weights, magnets, clamps, bolts, screws or rivets should always be considered. Another approach is to control the flow of heat by cooling with chills or copper heat sinks.

Thermal expansion and misalignment of joints tend to be more of a problem with jointing methods that employ a torch; the reason for this is due to the amount of heat absorbed by the metal before the weld area is hot enough to create a join. As an example, consider a simple plug weld formed between two sheets of 20swg. This is more likely to go awry if the top sheet is allowed to lift away – which is a real possibility with the flame from a torch. Whichever method you opt for, it will pay you to use clamps or temporary screws to hold the sheets as close together as possible. A lesser-known problem with this type of joint is simply caused by leaning on the panels with the Mig torch, which can lead to one panel riding over the other.

HOW DOES HEAT DISTORTION RELATE TO WELDING?

Here are three explanations for heat distortion in metal – all of which are true, but one or more may be more applicable to what you are doing at any particular time. (We will frame these explanations in terms of sheet metal, but this also applies to rods, bars and angle sections.)

1. Sheet steel is not naturally smooth. The flattened state in which we buy it is produced by rolling, which imparts stresses and surface tension which hold the sheet level. If you simply annealed the sheet it would 'normalize' and return to a more wobbly state; consider the heat-distorted area to have been simply annealed.

2. Distortion can be considered as uneven expansion and contraction of the different pieces during the welding process. Successive welds will fix each part to its neighbour when it is out of line due to uneven expansion. Imagine laying two 600m × 100m sheets of 20swg steel together so that they touch along one edge, and scribe marks across the join at 1-inch intervals. Then take a gas or Mig torch and place a 6mm tack weld across at any point along that seam. Continue tacking at random nine more times. Would you now expect the marks scribed across the seam to match up? As each weld was formed, so the sheets would have expanded due to the heat; the precise degree of expansion would have depended on many factors that are unlikely to have been exactly the same for each sheet. Likewise, as each weld cooled it would

have contracted; again the stresses on each side of the joint are unlikely to have been exactly similar.

3. Weld is metal which is molten and therefore expanded. As the liquid metal cools and hardens, it will contract. As it does so, it will try to pull together the pieces that have been joined. This must be accounted for or braced against. In some cases, particularly when working with cast items, a joint may fail or crack due to contraction. Preheating or controlled cooling may help.

4. Molten metal is liquid and as such has no tensile or load-bearing strength. Do not expect molten or red-hot metal to support its own weight or the weight of anything else. It would be wrong to confuse a structural failure or collapse with heat distortion. Many structures or components rely as much on their shape and on the surface tension that is imparted during pressing or drawing (as in wire) as they do from their mass or bulk. Heating will remove surface tension, thus weakening many component parts. Planishing, forging or tempering may be required to replace lost strength. Though many modern grades of alloy steel will return to full strength when cooled, the joining material (i.e. Mig wire or welding rod) will often not match the properties of the parent metal. For this reason, the repair or modification of safety-critical components such as vehicle suspension parts or alloy wheels cannot be recommended.

If you attempted to cut and rejoin a leaf-spring from an old cart or vehicle, the temper of the spring would be lost in the area where it was heated. Should you then attempt to use the spring in this condition, it would probably work-harden, then break or collapse at the joint. Building up this area with additional material in an attempt to gain strength would probably have the opposite effect, by creating a stress point instead.

Hammer welding techniques have been used over the years to reinstate lost tensility in panel work. Usually with these methods, a small area is welded and immediately dressed to shape using a hammer and dolly. Hammer welding is most successful when used with gas or Tig welding, as these pure fusion techniques do not create a build-up of material at the weld site in the way that Mig does. Also Mig uses a grade of steel wire that is harder than most of the jobs which it is used to repair.

WHAT CAN YOU DO TO LESSEN DISTORTION?

While a certain amount of distortion is inevitable, in some cases there are techniques you can use to prevent the worst of it, such as chills, Coldfront paste and copper heat sinks and backing bars.

Chills

Wet rags placed either side of a weld will greatly reduce heat absorption of a panel. If access allows another pair of chills to the rear, that would reduce it even further. Damp cloths are a cheap low-tech method of heat control – but beware that quenching a panel while it is in its expanded state will prevent it contracting to its original dimension.

Coldfront Paste

Coldfront is a proprietary ceramic paste that is used to protect items from heat damage. The product is cheap and reusable, it lasts for years and really does work. It is used in situations where for example a piece of trim cannot be removed, but would be damaged by the heat conducted through a panel. By placing a wall of the paste in line to block the flow of heat, or slathering the thing up with it, you can then weld away safe in the knowledge that your trim will remain cold.

COLDFRONT DEMONSTRATION

A popular demonstration of Coldfront was to place a big dollop of the paste on the palm of one hand and into this sit a copper coin. The coin was then heated with a torch until it glowed red. The hand remained cool and comfortable. Please don't try this for safety reasons, but it does actually work.

DISTORTION CONTROL

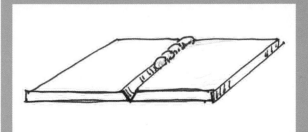

A simple butt joint with chamfer to aid penetration.

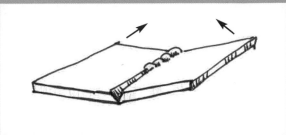

When welded from one side only, the joint will tend to close towards the weld as it cools.

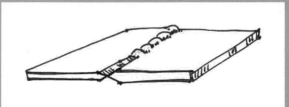

The double chamfer will lead to less distortion as one side pulls against the other.

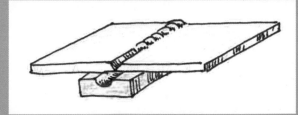

A backing bar will help to keep things in line and can reduce heat-soak into the surrounding metal.

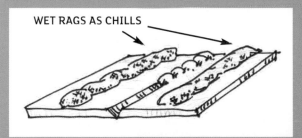

WET RAGS AS CHILLS

Chills used to reduce heat-soak and distortion.

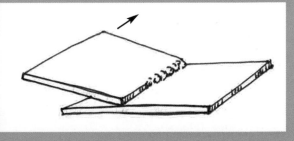

Lap joint welded from one edge only may open due to uneven stress. Close towards the weld as it cools.

Even stress from welding on both sides: a capillary brazed joint would avoid this problem.

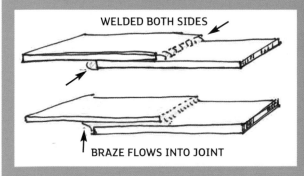

WELDED BOTH SIDES

BRAZE FLOWS INTO JOINT

Vee cut aids penetration.

Single and second run.

Cross-section shows depth of penetration.

Heat Sinks

In days gone by, boiler-makers would employ sheets or billets of copper to duct away unwanted heat. Many panel beaters use wet paper towel wrapped in foil to protect fuel pipes and other objects that might be damaged by weld spatter. Aluminium sheet is a more robust alternative.

Backing Bars

Grooved copper backing bars will help to reduce distortion by supporting both sides of a seam as you weld. At a push you could use steel bars, but be careful not to fuse the backing bar to the weld.

Heavy plates.

Angle section used as a brace.

*Left: Root run and
zig-zag from 130
amp Mig.*

EXTREMES OF DOMESTIC WELDER

*Right: Depth of penetration
can be seen.*

WELDING HEAVY OBJECTS

Large or heavy objects that soak up a lot of heat are particularly difficult to weld. In some cases a perfectly good weld will appear to have been formed, but will then be seen to crack as it cools. cast-iron/steel items or bronze casting are often best brazed rather than welded. Silver solder is commonly used to braze bronze statuary if damaged or when replacing a missing piece. The problem is compounded when one of the pieces being attached is considerably less massive than the other.

Preheating

If the object in question is small enough, you might consider preheating it in an oven. This works for items such as an HGV brake drum – but obviously will not do for your average Rodin. Warming the statue with a blowtorch or acetylene torch is the alternative, but this must be carried out with care to prevent discoloration or further damage. The more massive part will conduct more heat, so concentrate the flame on the larger of the sections to be joined. When preheating with a torch it is important to understand the difference between 'a lot of heat', and 'a high temperature'. You need to think in terms of 'thermal inertia' which is to say the ability for the heat to spread in the manner which works for us when trying to create the joint.

Controlled Cooling

As we know, molten metal is expanded and must contract as it cools. We can mitigate against the problem of cracking to some extent by controlling the rate at which the job cools. Continue to add heat to the object after it has been welded/brazed, concentrating the flame on the joint itself and the larger mass of metal. Remember that the object here is to control the cooling rate and not to continue increasing the heat.

Studding

Studding is used to improve strength when joining cast items. Drill, tap and insert a stud or bolt into one or both faces of the join, weld-in the stud and then fill the joint in the usual way. The stud will penetrate deeper than the fusion. In the case of brazing, where only surface bonding will occur, studding may improve strength considerably, as it will also increase the surface area of the join.

PRE-EMPTING DISTORTION

If we know how much, and in which direction a weld is likely to distort, we can in theory account for it by setting our component parts slightly out of line and watch as they correct themselves as the weld cools. This is a good theory, so when producing a batch of identical joins you might invest your time with trial welds. Measure the degree of distortion and account for it in subsequent production.

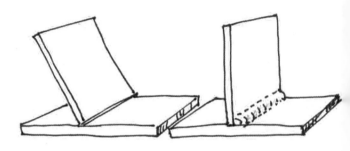

Pre-empting distortion – the weld pulls the metal into the correct position as it cools and hardens.

PRE-EMPTING MOVEMENT

In general, most welders will opt to brace against distortion. During fabrication it is standard practice to clamp pieces together firmly, prior to actually welding up. Mole grips and G-cramps are invaluable – as are odd bits of angle iron and box-section that are used to keep things square.

Vee Cut

Veeing the joint will allow for a stronger joint or for grinding flat afterwards. The exact placement and amount of weld will be governed by each application, and the degree of strength required.

*Example of heavy fabricated bracket using angleiron and box-section
to brace weld – be careful not to fix braces or clamps with weld.*

Chop saw.

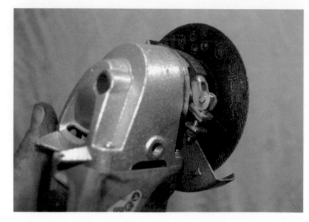

115 × 0.8 cutting disc.

Hard, flap cutting and fibre discs.

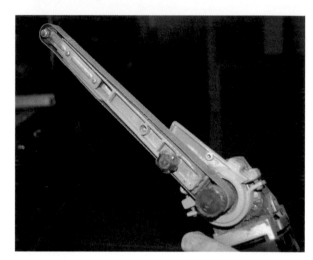

Belt sander.

Magnetic blocks.

Magnets.

CHAPTER 14

Steel Construction

In this chapter we discuss common tools, materials and techniques used for creating joints in steel construction.

TOOLS

All these materials can be cut with a hacksaw or with a cutting disc on an angle grinder. If you intend to cut a lot of this material, you would do well to invest in a chop saw, as accurately cut mitre joints will speed up your working hugely. For major projects a chop saw will save many hours and headaches by easily creating accurate and tidy joints. An 0.8mm disc on your angle grinder will cut through most profiles accurately, but care must be taken not to twist the blade or it will shatter.

MATERIALS AND HOW TO FORM JOINTS WITH THEM

Tubes, box-section, angle iron and steel bar are relatively cheap and very versatile.

Becoming friendly with your local steel fabricators is a good way of gaining access to all of your steel requirements at nigh on trade prices. His dumpster will provide all manner of goodies which would otherwise be prohibitively expensive, and he can carry out any production processes which are beyond you – at a reasonable price.

You may also find a local supplier who specializes in small amounts of steel. These people will cut and deliver anything and will beat your DIY superstore hands down. Trade materials are often supplied in 8-metre lengths – while buying these sizes would prove cheaper, most of us will not be able to handle or cut such quantities. Your supplier will charge a nominal amount to supply and cut the

Various clamps.

Hi-tech clamp.

G-cramps.

Plastic clamps for assembly work.

steel into more manageable lengths. You will find that a lot of this steel work will come to you covered in a light millscale, which will need to be cleaned off at the point where it is to be welded. Failure to remove the scale would result in poor fusion.

Angle Iron

Angle iron is actually made of mild steel. A traditional fabrication material which is able to keep its shape over long lengths, this quality and its relative light weight makes angle iron ideal for fabrication

work. This material can easily be mated to metal sheet, timber and concrete or masonry. It is available in a wide range of sizes, thickness, and profiles. U-channel and C-section are also popular. These profiles can be curved by your local steel fabricator.

Right-Angle Joint

Shown on pages 133–135 are three methods of creating a right-angle joint. The first is a simple overlap, the second is a mitre and the third is a notched flush joint.

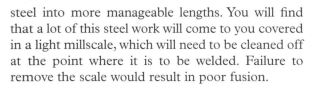

WHAT DO YOU CALL IT?

Q: There is always the possibility of confusion when talking about metal profiles. For example, do you ask for 'wire' or 'rod'?

A: State the dimension and call it 'round-section'.

Q: Another common mix-up is with flat metal – is it 'sheet' or is it 'plate'?

A: State the metal thickness and specify 'flat steel'.

In both cases, the break is at about 3mm. Below this thickness we have 'wire' and 'sheet', and above 3mm, it is commonly called 'rod' and 'plate'; but the terms remain interchangeable to some degree in common parlance.

Tube fixed to plate.

EXAMPLES OF STEEL SECTIONS

Plates set in position for welding.

Single pass near, and second pass overweld behind.

After grinding, second pass of weld produces neat corner profile.

OPEN CORNER JOINT

Square Tube or Box-Section

Box-section or square tube is another useful form of steel which is very easy to turn into structures with great strength and rigidity. Box-sections are available in a wide range of sizes and wall thickness. Box-section provides many of the qualities of conventional round tubing but is far easier to joint and brace. Additional corner web adds huge strength to joints. Internal or external sleeves can be used when extending box-section.

Round-Section Tube

This traditional material has been used to make pretty much everything over the years. It is obviously not possible to create a flush 'butted right-angle' joint using round tube. At a push you can fill

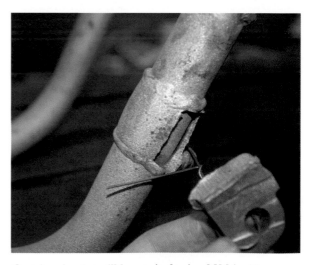

Cast-iron bracket will be repaired using MMA with matching cast-iron rod. Brazing should be considered as an alternative.

Set piece in place and clamp – check angle.

Internal view.

Initial weld – take care not to weld the clamp on.

Weld continued around joint – exact amount of weld is governed by strength required.

Internal view after external welding has been completed.

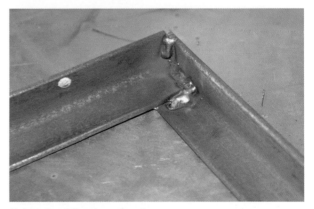

Internal welding is optional.

FORMATION OF SIMPLE OVERLAP CORNER JOINT USING ANGLE SECTION

Mitre joint set up with clamp.

Internal view of mitre.

Internal welding gives strength.

External view after welding and grinding off.

FORMATION OF MITRED CORNER JOINT USING ANGLE SECTION

the gap with weld – this works best if the piece you are butting is considerably smaller than the other. To create accurately angled joints requires a 'notcher'. The notcher is a jig that holds a 'tank-cutter' – this allows the tube to be set at any angle and is then cut by the saw to accommodate its counterpart.

Accurate fabrication also requires a jig to locate and brace the tubing whilst it is being welded. A piece of L-section can be used as a jig for creating simple joints along the length of a square or round tube. Use of internal or external sleeves will make joining tube section easier and stronger.

Shown on page 138 is the Dresda jig which, as you can see, is made of heavy gauge box-section and has over the last twenty-five and more years, been used to produce hundreds of classic 'Triton' motorcycles.

Cut and Weld Joint in Flat Plate

Shown here is a bit of plate which has been cut partway through with an 0.8mm disc. The plate was then folded to the correct angle and welded. This piece was then fixed to a section of tube and used as a jack extension.

Joint is created by cutting notch into one piece with 0.8mm disc on grinder.

Welding completed – any gaps prior to welding will aid penetration and therefore strength.

Joint after grinding off.

Internal welding is optional, but will improve strength if front is ground flush.

FLUSH NOTCHED CORNER JOINT USING ANGLE SECTION

Rod Fixed to Bar-Section

This is a typical joint which might be used to produce a gate of security grate. Here we have drilled halfway into the bar, so as to give the rod a positive location. We then welded the rod in place. A stronger and neater alternative might be to drill through the bar and weld from the other side. Braze would also have been an option, as the brass could

Profile of square tube lends itself to this type of joint.

Mitre joint has been veed to aid penetration.

FORMING A MITRE JOINT
WITH BOX-SECTION

Outside seam is welded to hold location.

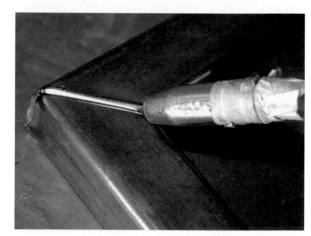

Preparing to weld into vee.

Weld penetrates into vee to produce sound joint.

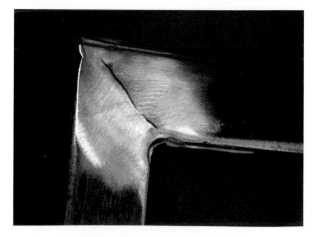

Mitre joint is flush after grinding off.

Corner fillet adds hugely to strength – this weld can also be ground flush.

Corner fillet added to non-veed mitre joint – note blunting of corner peak to account for internal weld.

Round tubes do not lend themselves to this type of joint.

Gap in joint is built up with weld.

Round tube mitre joint would benefit from veeing.

Tack to locate mitre. internal weld is difficult to remove with grinder.

Complete weld is untidy due to ever-changing angle – practice is required.

Notched joint is flush fitting and gives positive location.

Notcher is essentially a drill-powered tank-cutter mounted in a variable jig.

External sleeve adds strength and aids alignment.

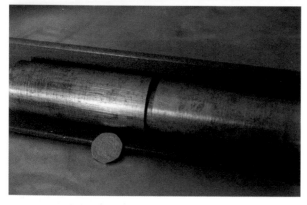

Internal sleeve joint can be ground flush – angle section used as jig.

The Dresda jig has produced classic 'Triton' motorcycles for decades.

Square tubes sleeved together allow adjustment in construction.

Partial cut through plate allows for accurate folding.

After setting to correct angle the fold is welded to restore strength.

Rod set into locating hole in bar to create security grating.

Mig welding joint – brazing would also work well here.

Vehicle bodywork.

CHAPTER 15

Vehicle Bodywork

Here we will be dealing with sheet metal work as it relates to car panel fixing and restoration.

WORKING WITH LIGHT GAUGE SHEET

Vehicle bodywork is all about thin steel sheets, nominally 20swg and 18swg (0.9mm and 1.2mm) for panel and chassis respectively. When dealing with motor factors or paint suppliers, don't be surprised to find anything from 22swg (0.7mm) to 17swg (1.4mm) being sold as 20swg.

This material tends to come with a light anodized coating which will burn off without any special cleaning (in the recent past a light coat of oil was the norm). Any oily film present will need to be removed immediately prior to working – apart from making a terrible mess, it will not allow pencil marking and will spit when welded. Avoid galvanized steel which will spit and burn terribly and gives off a toxic smoke.

Mark any cut lines with a scribe or pencil – fold lines and other details should only be marked with a soft pencil, as a scribe might break the surface which could then cause a fracture or weakness when folding.

NEW MEETS OLD

When joining new steel to old, you may notice differences in the resilience or springiness. It is often said that older cars were made from far better metal than their modern counterparts, but the truth is that over the years steels have been formulated to 'flow' during the pressing process, and many vehicle panels from the 1970s and 1980s feel rather 'dead'.

Rusty or pitted panels will behave in a different manner to fresh new steel, and working on real cars is obviously not the same as practising on a bench. Experience shows us that getting a feel for light gauge steel under ideal conditions is a better approach than jumping in at the deep end. Real life welding applications often involve craning your hand overhead to join damp, rusty and contaminated metal to pristine fresh steel.

TECHNIQUES AND EXERCISES

For these examples we have used a 103 amp Cebora Mig. But whichever method of welding you choose could equally be applied to the following exercises.

Welding with Small Pieces of 20swg

The first exercise is to simply draw a line of weld in a single thickness of metal. This exercise is designed

---

PATCHING FLOOR PANELS

It used to be said that a good welder could 'join rusty air'. With this in mind, you might consider getting to grips with a few MOT failures. Making and fitting patches to rotten floor panels will sharpen up your skills no end.

Once you have mastered working with new metal on the bench, move on to fitting the odd wing. This will demand that you work at different heights and angles joining new metal to old.

Repairing rusty old cars is not glamorous, but is the best possible grounding in the skills needed to restore classic vehicles.

Preparing to weld.

Short run shows initial build-up followed by good penetration.

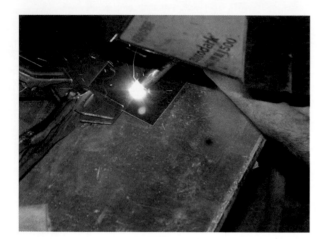

Continued welding.

Hot weld is quite flat, suggesting good penetration.

SIMPLE EXERCISE: RUNNING A LINE OF WELD ALONG SHEET OF 20SWG

to give you control – too slow and you will burn a hole, while too fast will result in poor penetration. Turn the piece over and see how the heat has come through.

Simple Butt Weld

This is similar to the previous exercise, but the gap will mean more control is required. If using gas or Tig, the aim is to use only the metal of the sheet – any holes will require additional filler rod. A run of overlapping small welds will tend to create less heat build-up and so lessen the chance of distortion or burning through. We have deliberately blown a hole so as to show how easy it is to then bridge it.

Overlap Joint

This one should be a tad easier, as the overlap absorbs heat more evenly and with far less risk of burning through. Uneven heating will result in the top layer lifting – use clamps as required.

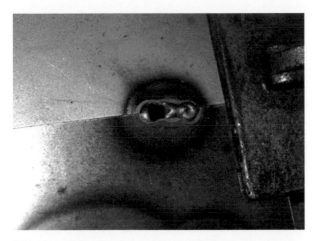

This shows how easy it is to blow a hole due to heat build.

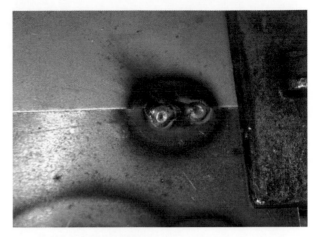

And how easy it is to fill any holes.

Continue with 'pulsed' welding to lessen risk of burning.

Completed weld holds residual heat.

Overlapping studs of weld form 'string of pearls'.

BUTT JOINT IN 20SWG

This shows stepped lap formed in panels.

Earth attached and ready to weld.

Welding commenced.

A single continuous weld.

Lap allows for confident hot welding.

LAPPED JOINT

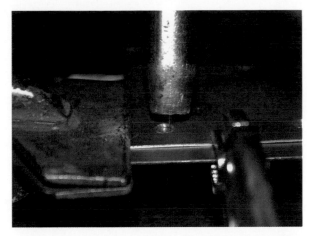

Holes punched on sheet for plug welds with torch held ready.

Torch is held steady during process and 'stirred' to ensure complete flow across hole.

Second weld has been stirred, where first was not – note gap. The weld is incomplete in first weld.

Heat penetration on underside of stud welds.

Plug braze (see Gas Welding, Chapter 6).

FORMING PLUG WELDS

Exercise pieces ready.

Correct angle of torch is crucial.

Welding demands even movement across seam.

Uneven movement or poor aim will result in untidy weld.

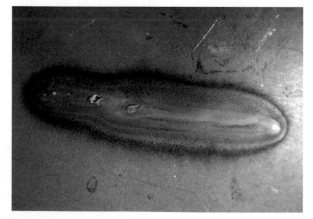

Three-way heat-soak of this type of joint can lead to poor penetration.

CORNER FILLET JOINT

**OPPOSITE:
EXTERNAL CORNER JOINT**

Metal set up for external corner using magnets.

Initial weld is tentative.

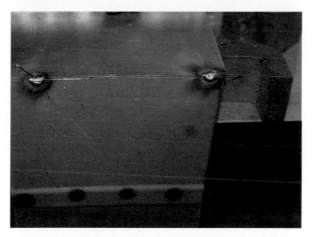

Tacks will prevent movement during welding.

Further welding must be undertaken with caution and a view to heat build-up.

Pausing will allow heat to dissipate, as will pulsing the welder.

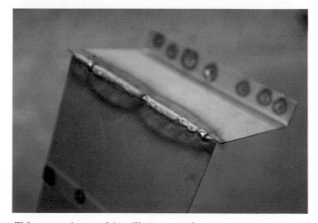

Take your time and it will come good.

Plug Weld

Punch or drill a row of holes 4–6mm along the edge of one piece of metal, and lay it over the other. Clamp the pieces together and aim to fill each hole while bonding it to the lower piece. This exercise is best suited to Mig welding and any of the brazing techniques.

Internal Corner Fillet Joint

This is a right-angle joint and needs a close fit of the parts to create a neat weld. Any gap is likely to lead to burning, due to uneven heat absorption. Note the way that the heat has distorted the lower piece of metal.

You could use a simple butt joint.

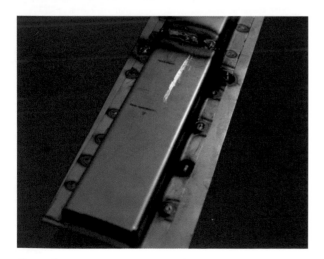

Stepped overlap section is prepared – this allows for hotter weld and some adjustment.

External Corner Joint: Open Corner

This is a key skill. Once you feel confident with this exercise, try making a small box. The ultimate test is to make very small boxes with welded edges. These are dipped into water to check for a good seal.

External Corner Made Easier

Here is a good way to make life easier – having first mastered the hard way. When forming a piece which will be joined with an external corner type joint, leave an extra couple of mm and turn this over to the correct angle in order to receive its counterpart. The extra metal will allow for far more confident welding with a greatly reduced risk of burning through. The vestigial flange also provides a purchase for clamps.

Tacking

When setting up any type of joint, you will often find it beneficial to tack the metal into place. Strategically placed small welds will prevent mis-location as the run of weld progresses. In much the same manner clamps, rivets or self-tapping screws can be used to support and locate a panel or section

BOX-SECTION JOINT

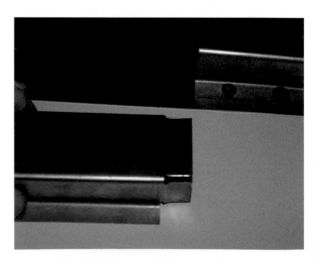

After welding the joint can safely be ground off flush.

Vestigial flange allows for much more confident welding…

…and the use of clamps.

Huge heat build can be seen in weld – but little distortion.

EXTERNAL CORNER JOINT MADE EASIER

Smooth continuous weld.

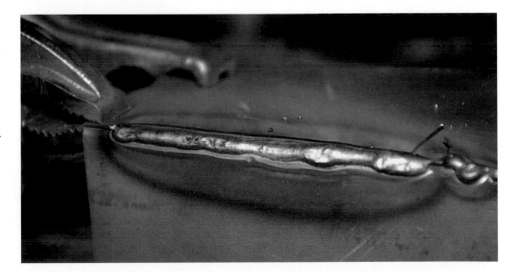

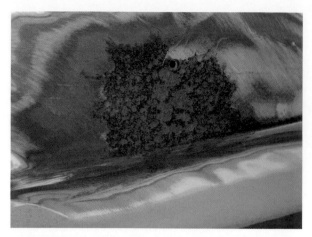

A suitable patch of rot for treatment.

A conveniently sized disc is drawn out…

…and cut from fresh metal.

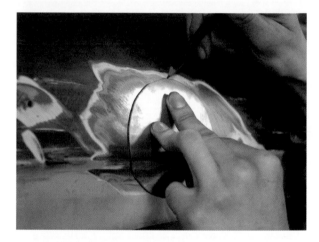

After shaping the disc is marked onto panel.

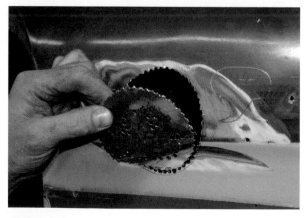

Drill inside of circle and nip between holes to remove grot before filing.

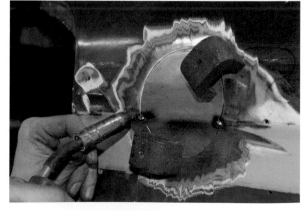

Patch is sat flush and strategically tacked.

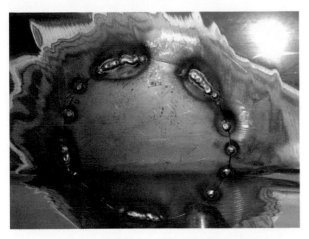

Keep tacks apart as far as possible – until you run out of space.

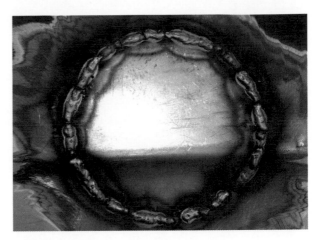

Fill in between tacks with overlapping studs – work across panel to minimize heat build-up.

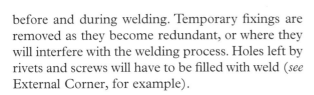

Grind off with care to remove only excess metal.

CIRCULAR PATCH IN MID-PANEL REPAIRS

before and during welding. Temporary fixings are removed as they become redundant, or where they will interfere with the welding process. Holes left by rivets and screws will have to be filled with weld (*see* External Corner, for example).

Circular Patch

This is an old boilermaker's trick, which can be put to good use on vehicle panels using gas Mig or Tig. The idea is that a circular patch will expand and contract more evenly than one with corners. It's also a perfect introduction to the strategy of placing welds where the heat can dissipate, before the next

is applied – this is a key principal of distortion control in bodywork and is relevant to every job involving an exterior panel.

This exercise is best practised on an old panel, preferably one with a curved profile. As your skill develops you can apply this technique to corner sections and mid-panel areas that feature details such as swage lines.

Select an appropriate bit of rotten metal to replace. Mark out and cut a suitable disc of new steel. Form the disc to match the profile of the panel. Scribe around the new disc. Remove the rotten metal by first drilling a series of holes inside the

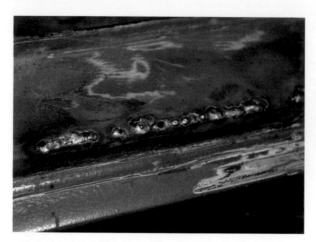

Displacing rust with Mig weld.

Be prepared to blow a few holes in the process. Build a wall of weld around before bridging.

marked line, then cut between the holes with snips or a hacksaw. Clean up the hole to match exactly, and fit the patch into the gap so that it sits flush.

Tack the new disc around the circle with regard to heat dissipation – which is to say, space your welds as far apart as possible, so the welds reach about 30mm apart. You will need to fill the spaces between them, using overlapping spots of weld and again keeping each run as far apart as you can.

When the excess weld is removed, the finished patch should be nearly invisible.

Box-Section Overlap Joint

Chassis members, sills, out riggers and pillars will benefit from strong and accurate jointing. This method not only promotes hot confident welding, but also allows for a degree of fine adjustment without creating a gap.

Mark up and cut your repair section with 13mm extra. Remove anything that will not lap neatly, such as the edges, and split all the corners. Form a step with a joddler/joggler or edge-set. Tuck the new metal under the old and weld into the hollow next to the seam. When the excess is ground off the seam should be flush.

RUST REPAIRS
Displacing Light Rust with Weld

It is not unusual to use Mig weld to displace a bit of

grot, if the base metal is sound enough to cope with the process.

Experience will teach you that rusty metal will accept weld in a different manner to sound metal, but with practice your ability to repair poorer and poorer base metal will improve. Listen for a slightly 'soggy' sound as the welder hits corroded metal. Pitting can be replaced with Mig weld in some cases, although you do have to be prepared to blow a few holes whilst trying.

To bridge across a hole, first build a wall of weld around it, where you know the metal to be sound. Work inward from the wall, gradually allowing the

Cobalt drills are prone to blunting, but can be sharpened on a bench grinder.

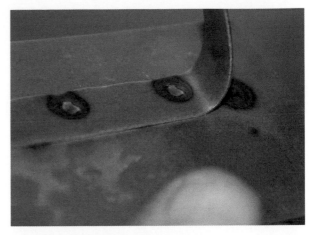

Drill to depth of one layer of metal.

Lift gash metal sharply to form handle.

'Wiggle' the handle to fracture ring around central nugget of weld.

Use mole grips to aid this process.

HOW TO UNDO A SPOT WELD

Use of carpenter's chisel to split around weld leaving central nugget.

Illustrates benefit and limitation of spot welder.

heat to soak, or you will be chasing an ever-increasing gap. Try not to build upwards or you will have large amounts of excess metal to grind off.

In some instances, where you have access to both sides of a hole, you can sit a piece of copper behind the gap and build weld around the periphery. The weld cannot adhere to the copper, so you should be able to use it as a support.

Grinding Off

The key to successful grinding is to stroke rather than dig – use a hard grinding disc only to remove the outer material. Then use a flexible fibre disc or flap-disc for the removal of material nearer to the panel itself. Take great care not to remove any of the actual panel or this will become thin and weak. Power-files or belt sanders are useful for getting into corners and awkward areas.

MOT REPAIRS

When carrying out rust repairs for an MOT test, there are a few things to bear in mind.

Firstly, the MOT tester is probably a mechanic, and he may not share your understanding of vehicle structure. Whatever the rationale behind your chosen method of repair, it is his judgement as to whether the car passes or not.

Brazing techniques are not acceptable for structural and chassis repairs. Box members and structural sections must be continuously welded, and your welding should be presented without sealer or any sort of covering which might conceal poor repairs.

Many floor repairs and chassis box sections such as outriggers can be fixed from inside the car. The only problem with this is that the MOT man will probably only see your work from outside and could be mistaken into thinking that it is less substantial than it really is. A good example of this is an outrigger which is stud-welded through the original spot-weld holes, which may not show new weld under the car other than where it meets the chassis rail or sill. Welding overhead demands different grips of the torch and a new respect for pain.

UNDOING RESISTANCE SPOT WELDS

The resistance spot-weld is made up of a central nugget of fused material which is surrounded by a ring of metal that has been heated but not to the point of melting. This ring is softer than both the nugget and the normal metal of the panel. Careful drilling and removal can allow a panel to be refixed using stud-welds.

Drill Out the Weld

Use a 'cobalt' drill to cut out the weld by centring it on the middle of the dimple and aim to remove only one layer of metal. Cobalt-type drills are prone to losing their centre spurs. Judicious use of the bench grinder can bring even the most tired back to perfect shape.

Wiggle Off the Weld

If you remove the bulk of the panel, leaving a row of welds on the mounting flange in place, you can then lift one end of this strip to form a handle. Pull sharply on this handle, up to the first weld. Next, 'wiggle' the handle until the soft metal surrounding the weld fractures leaving only the central nugget in place.

Use a Chisel

If the welds prove to be stubborn, you can use a carpenter mortise chisel to split between the two panels. Aim to cut through the ring around the nugget.

Gas welding requires practice and more practice.

Glossary

AC (alternating current) electrical current used in Tig welding when fusing aluminium and some light alloys – an alternating current is superimposed over the welding current to ensure a continuous arc; emissions from this can damage other electrical devices and interfere with communications equipment.

annealing process used to remove work-hardening and brittleness cause by overworking a piece of metal, by heating it to the point where the crystals 'normalize' (take on a random arrangement).

arc welding any method of welding in which the heat for the process is provided by electricity that is forced to jump a gap between a torch and the work piece. In most of these techniques the electrode is consumed as a deposit of metal on the work surface. The exception to this rule is Tig.

blowback a minor detonation within gas welding equipment, usually the torch nozzle.

brass 'welding' a metal-joining process like brazing – but one in which the rod is melted directly onto the joint to form a shoulder or reinforcement.

braze to join metal using brass as a filler or bonding material; this term can also refer to any method involving a torch or 'brazier'.

brazing a metal-joining process like soldering, but needing higher temperature to be activated, commonly using a brass-based alloy rod, in which the brass is 'flowed' by capillary action into the joint; the heat can be provided by a flame or electrical arc, although tongs, an oven or an iron can also be employed.

bronze 'welding' like brazing, but employing a bronze-based rod; bronze/brass are defined by their respective copper content.

buttering layers of good-quality weld applied to each face of a joint before the actual joining, often with a mass of cheaper material.

earth lead/clamp a lead or clamp (more correctly called 'power return lead') attached to the workpiece to complete a circuit with the welder; in some cases (e.g. Tig) the 'earth' will actually be positive (or live), in which case the torch is in fact the earth.

electrode the live component of any welding torch: in MMA it is a consumable rod or stick clamped to the torch; in Mig it is the copper tip through which the consumable wire is passed; in Tig it is a tungsten rod held in the torch.

filler rod/material welding rod or thin off-cuts used to bridge gaps or holes.

flashback arrestors device fitted inline with gas equipment to prevent the flame from travelling to the bottles.

flux a chemical (often acidic) used to clean a joint or remove oxides during soldering or welding; fluxes often aid the flow of a solder or braze by 'wetting' the surface and reducing surface tension; all fluxes and their fumes are toxic.

flux-cored describes solders or Mig wire containing a flux, which is released during the joining process.

gasless Mig a welding method utilizing a flux-cored wire which releases a shielding gas when it short-circuits with the workpiece; well suited to outdoor work in which a normal gas might be blown away (also known as flux-cored shielded arc welding).

HAZ (heat affected zone) The area immediately surrounding a weld in which the metal is altered at a molecular or crystalline level. In this area surface tension will be lost (also known as area of thermal disruption).

LPG liquid petroleum gas.

mapp gas a form of LPG which can be used as a fuel gas for welding or soldering.

Mig (metal inert gas welding) a method of arc welding in which an inert gas is used to displace oxygen from the weld area; the most suitable method of welding for most non- or semi-professional applications.

MMA (manual metal arc welding) is the simplest method of electrical arc welding. A consumable electrode is short-circuited to create an arc in which metal from the stick is transferred onto the workpiece (also known as stick welding).

oxy-acetylene gas brazing a method of joining metal by use of a flame which is hot enough to melt a brass or bronze alloy rod to the point where it will bond with the surface of another metal.

oxy-acetylene gas welding a method of joining metal by use of a flame which is hot enough to heat a localized area to melting point, so that two pieces can be fused.

oxy-mapp gas welding/brazing an economical alternative to oxy-acetylene welding for the small-time user; mapp gas burns hotter than propane.

pre-fluxed describes welding or brazing rods with a coating of flux material that has been bonded to the outside; in some cases grooves will be formed into the rod into which flux has then been set.

slag the residue from flux or welding processes, which may interfere with successive weld or impair joint strength.

solder a piece of metal, originally lead or tin, in the form of rod or wire, which is heated to melting point and thereby used to join many metals – commonly copper, brass and steel; less toxic alternatives are now available.

studding a method of increasing penetration by drilling and tapping a hole into the face to be repaired; into this is screwed a stud which is then welded in and incorporated into successive runs of weld material.

Tig (tungsten inert gas welding) a form of arc welding in which an inert gas is used to displace oxygen from the weld area; tungsten here refers to the electrode material.

tinning the process of applying solder to a piece before creating a joint; two 'tinned' pieces are then brought together and reheated (also known as pre-tinning).

welding in its truest sense, a process by which two or more pieces of metal are fused to become one, without adding any foreign alloy.

Useful Information

Having read this book, the reader should now be in a position to decide which welding methods best suit his needs, and be confident enough to make a safe start. Welding is a subject that can never be fully mastered by any one person; there will always be more tricks to learn.

A trawl of the internet will throw up many options for books DVDs and welding courses, but we would advise caution when deciding where to get further instruction. A book that gives perfect instruction on how to weld North Sea gas pipes is probably not going to be much help if you want to make garden furniture. We would suggest any search be narrowed by specifying which welding method you are wishing to study further.

We would strongly recommend that you take instruction from an experienced practitioner, although the following DVD and books are recommended:

- Gardiner, David *Bodywork Restoration Tutorial* DVD (metalshapingzone.com)
- Thaddeus, Martin *How to Restore Classic Car Bodywork* (Veloce Enthusiast's Restoration Manual series)
- Wakeford, R.E. *Sheet Metal Work* (Workshop Practice)

Contour Bodycraft (Tel: 01406 370504) is the acknowledged leader in panel fabrication skills courses. You may also find that your local college can offer a more general restoration course.

TOOLS AND EQUIPMENT

- BOC publishes a product catalogue that covers most of the popular welding methods in reasonable detail and gives a good idea of the material options open to you. www.boc-gases.com
- Weld UK has a good website for most of the stuff you may need. A chat with the proprietor will prove invaluable. www.welduk.com
- *Practical Classics Magazine* (Bauer) and *Classic Monthly* (Future Publishing) both cover the world of old cars and will often review welding equipment, as well as carrying advertisements for welding and metalwork equipment.
- Frost Restorer Equipment can supply anything to do with car restoration.
- LB Restorations sell only high-quality restoration tools.
- Namrick can supply small or large quantities of all types of fixing and fastening goods by mail order.

Index